BEYOND
THE HIGHLIGHT REEL

Navigating the Illusion of Online Success

Shikta Mohanty

Table of Contents

Introduction

In today's digital age, the allure of building an online business or influencer brand is strong. The promise of being your own boss, working from home, and earning a six-figure income is an enticing prospect for many. Social media platforms have made it easier than ever to share your story and build a following. However, the reality of building an online business or influencer brand is often much more challenging than it appears.

In this chapter, we will explore the challenges and opportunities of building an online business or influencer brand. We will delve into the difficulties of generating revenue from social media, the pressures of maintaining an online presence, and the toll it can take on your mental health. We will also discuss the importance of prioritizing your well-being and seeking support when you need it.

Lisa's Story: Thrive in the Digital Age

Lisa had always been an ambitious person. However, as a single mother of two, she struggled to find the time and resources to pursue her goals. Her job as a customer service representative paid enough to keep food on the table and a roof over their heads, but it left little room for extras. She often felt like she was barely keeping her head above water.

One day, while scrolling through her social media feed during her lunch break, Lisa stumbled upon an advertisement for an online business course. The ad promised that she could make thousands of dollars a month working from home in her spare time. Lisa felt a spark of hope. The idea of being able to start her own business and have the flexibility to work from home was particularly appealing.

As she delved deeper into the world of online business, Lisa began to feel more and more excited about the possibilities. She saw people sharing their success stories, earning six-figure incomes and traveling the world, all thanks to their online businesses. Lisa wanted a piece of that dream.

However, Lisa was also battling her own mental health issues. She had always struggled with anxiety and depression, and the stress of being a single mother had taken its toll on her. She found herself constantly worrying about her finances and her future, wondering if she was doing enough for her children.

Undeterred, Lisa began to research everything she could about online business. She read blog posts, watched video tutorials, and scoured social media for tips and advice. She started to get excited about the possibilities, imagining a future where she could work for herself and spend more time with her children.

Lisa soon discovered the world of Reels, where she saw people sharing snippets of their lives and earning money for it. She watched in awe as people showed off their luxurious lifestyles and shared their secrets to success. Lisa was hooked.

Determined to give it a try, Lisa began creating her own Reels, sharing snippets of her life as a single mother and offering advice on parenting and frugal living. She spent hours perfecting her content, researching hashtags, and engaging with her audience.

But despite all her hard work, Lisa struggled to gain traction. Her videos weren't getting many views, and the few comments she did receive were critical and unhelpful. She started to doubt herself, wondering if she had what it took to make it in the online world.

Lisa's mental health issues began to take a toll on her. She found herself struggling to balance her work, her children, and her online business. She was constantly exhausted and overwhelmed, and she found it difficult to focus on her goals.

Despite these challenges, Lisa didn't give up. She kept at it, determined to make her online business work. She began to explore other avenues for earning money online, such as freelance marketplaces. She started to build a website, learning as much as she could about web development and hosting.

As Lisa continued to work on her online business, she began to prioritize her mental health as well. She started seeing a therapist and practicing self-care. She also began to build a network of other online entrepreneurs and influencers, seeking advice and support from those who had gone before her.

Lisa's story is a common one in the world of online business and influencer marketing. It's easy to be drawn in by the promises of easy success and financial freedom, but the reality is often much more difficult. The online space is crowded and competitive, and success is never guaranteed. Building a successful online business or influencer brand requires hard work, dedication, and perseverance.

One of the biggest challenges of building an online business is generating revenue. While it's true that some influencers and online entrepreneurs can earn a six-figure income, the vast majority of people struggle to make a living from their online work. Social media platforms have made it easier than ever to build a following but monetizing that following can be a different story. The algorithms are constantly changing, and it can be difficult to keep up with the latest trends and best practices.

Another challenge of building an online business or influencer brand is the pressure to maintain an online presence. It's not enough to simply create good content; you also have to engage with your audience, respond to comments, and stay up to date on the latest social media trends. This can be exhausting, particularly for those who are already struggling with mental health issues.

Despite these challenges, many people are still drawn to the world of online business and influencer marketing. The flexibility and potential for financial freedom are too enticing to ignore. But it's important to approach this world with caution and realistic expectations. Building an online business takes time, effort, and a willingness to learn from both successes and failures.

In the following chapters, we will explore the various aspects of building an online business or influencer brand, including generating revenue, building a following, and maintaining your mental health. We will provide practical advice and insights from experienced online entrepreneurs and influencers, and we will discuss the importance of seeking support and taking care of yourself along the way. Whether you're just starting out or you're a seasoned pro, this book is for anyone who wants to navigate the online world with confidence and resilience.

Building an Online Business or Influencer Brand

Building an online business or influencer brand can take many different forms. In recent years, the rise of social media and digital platforms has made it easier than ever to establish an online presence and monetize your content. From making videos on social media platforms to publishing books on self-publishing platforms, selling products on e-Commerce platform, writing blogs, and freelancing on freelance platforms, there are many different ways to succeed in the online world.

In this section, we will explore the concept of building an online business or influencer brand in more detail. We will delve into the various challenges and opportunities associated with this field and provide practical advice on how to succeed. We will also discuss the different types of online businesses and influencer brands and provide examples of individuals who have achieved success in these areas.

The first step in building an online business or influencer brand is to define your niche. This means identifying a specific area of interest or expertise that you can focus on. Whether you're passionate about cooking, writing, graphic design, or web development, there are plenty of opportunities to find your niche and create engaging content that resonates with your audience.

Once you have identified your niche, the next step is to create a digital presence. This means building a website or creating social media profiles that showcase your brand and your content. Your digital presence should be cohesive and consistent, with a clear message and aesthetic that reflects your brand values.

One of the biggest challenges of building an online business or influencer brand is generating revenue. While it's true that some influencers and online entrepreneurs can earn a six-figure income, the vast majority of people struggle to make a living from their online work. Monetizing your online presence requires a combination of strategy and creativity. This might include selling digital products or services, offering sponsored content, or partnering with brands for affiliate marketing.

Making videos on platforms is one popular way to build an online following. These platforms allow you to showcase your creativity and personality and can be a great way to connect with your audience. However, creating high-quality video content can be time-consuming and requires some technical know-how.

Publishing books on self-publishing platforms is another way to establish yourself as an online influencer. Whether you're an expert in a particular field or have a unique story to share, self-publishing on some popular platforms can be a great way to reach a wider audience and earn passive income. However, it's important to note that writing and self-publishing a book takes time and effort, and success is never guaranteed.

Selling products on e-commerce platforms is yet another way to build an online business. Whether you're creating handmade goods or reselling products from a manufacturer, Some websites provides a platform to reach a massive audience and generate revenue. However, competition can be fierce, and it can be difficult to stand out in a crowded marketplace.

Blogging is another popular way to establish an online presence and build a following. By creating engaging, informative content, you can attract readers and build a community around your brand. However, it's important to note that blogging takes time and effort, and success often requires a long-term commitment.

Finally, freelancing on platforms can be a great way to monetize your skills and build a client base. Whether you're a writer, graphic designer, or web developer, there are plenty of opportunities to find work on these platforms. However, it's important to be aware of the challenges associated with freelancing, including finding consistent work and dealing with difficult clients.

It's important to note that building an online business or influencer brand is not a get-rich-quick scheme. It takes time and effort to establish a presence and gain a following. Success in this field requires dedication, perseverance, and a willingness to learn from both successes and failures.

Another challenge of building an online business or influencer brand is the pressure to maintain an online presence. In today's digital age, it's not enough to simply create good content; you also have to engage with your audience, respond to comments, and stay up-to-date on the latest social media trends. This can be exhausting, particularly for those who are already struggling with mental health issues.

In the following sections, we will explore each of these topics in more detail, providing practical advice and real-life examples of individuals who have succeeded in building an online business or influencer brand. We will also discuss the importance of prioritizing your mental health and seeking support when you need it. Whether you're just starting out or you're looking to take your online presence to the next level, this book is for anyone who wants to succeed in the digital age.

Allure of online success and how it can be deceiving

Building an online business or influencer brand is a journey that can be both exciting and challenging. While the allure of online success can be strong, it's important to acknowledge that the path to success is not always easy. In this section, we will discuss the allure of online success and how it can be deceiving.

Social media and digital platforms have created a culture of constant comparison and competition, where success is often measured in terms of likes, followers, and engagement. This can create a distorted view of success, one that is based more on appearances than on actual financial or professional success. The pressure to present a polished and perfect image online can lead to feelings of inadequacy and anxiety, as individuals struggle to live up to the expectations of their followers and peers.

In addition to the pressure to present a perfect image, the perception of success in the online world can be misleading. Many influencers and online entrepreneurs present a highly curated and filtered version of their lives, creating a false sense of success that can make it difficult for others to recognize the hard work and dedication that goes into building a successful online brand.

The allure of online success can also create unrealistic expectations, leading individuals to believe that building an online business or influencer brand is a quick and easy path to success. In reality, the path to success is often filled with challenges and setbacks, and requires a great deal of hard work, persistence, and dedication.

One of the biggest challenges of building an online business or influencer brand is generating revenue. While it's true that some influencers and online entrepreneurs can earn a six-figure income, the vast majority of people struggle to make a living from their online work. Monetizing your online presence requires a combination of strategy and creativity. This might include selling digital products or services, offering sponsored content, or partnering with brands for affiliate marketing.

Another challenge is the constant need to stay up-to-date with the latest trends and technologies. The online world is constantly evolving, and keeping up with these changes can be a full-time job in itself. This can create a sense of overwhelm and anxiety, as individuals struggle to stay on top of the latest developments and trends.

Perhaps one of the biggest challenges of building an online business or influencer brand is the pressure to be constantly "on." Social media and digital platforms have created a culture of instant gratification, where success is measured in real-time engagement and interaction. This can create a sense of pressure to be constantly connected and responsive, leading to burnout and fatigue.

Despite these challenges, building an online business or influencer brand can be incredibly rewarding. The ability to connect with a global audience and share your message with the world is a powerful thing, and can be a source of inspiration and motivation. By acknowledging the potential pitfalls of online success, and developing a realistic and sustainable plan for growth, individuals can navigate the online world with greater confidence and resilience.

The allure of online success can also create a sense of isolation and disconnection. While social media and digital platforms allow us to connect with people from all over the world, they can also create a sense of distance and detachment from our real-world communities. This can be especially true for individuals who work from home or spend a significant amount of time online.

The pressure to present a perfect image online can also create feelings of imposter syndrome and self-doubt. This is particularly true in the world of influencer marketing, where success is often measured in terms of followers and engagement rather than actual financial or professional success. The constant need to present a polished and curated image can lead to feelings of inadequacy and anxiety, as individuals struggle to live up to the expectations of their followers and peers.

One way to overcome these challenges is to cultivate a sense of authenticity and vulnerability in your online presence. This means being honest and transparent about the challenges and setbacks that you face, and sharing your journey with your audience in a real and meaningful way. By doing so, you can create a sense of connection and community with your followers, and build a more authentic and sustainable online brand.

Another way to overcome the challenges of online success is to develop a strong support network. This might include joining online communities and groups, seeking out mentorship and guidance from other successful online entrepreneurs, or working with a coach or therapist to address any mental health issues or challenges that arise.

Finally, it's important to remember that online success is not the only measure of success. Building a successful online business or influencer brand is just one path to success, and there are many different ways to achieve your goals and live a fulfilling life. By prioritizing your values and focusing on what truly matters to you, you can create a sense of purpose and meaning in your online work, and build a successful and sustainable online brand that reflects your unique talents and passions.

In the following sections, we will explore these themes in more detail, providing practical advice and real-life examples of individuals who have succeeded in building an authentic and sustainable online presence. Whether you're just starting out on your online journey, or you're looking to overcome the challenges of online success, this book is for anyone who wants to navigate the online world with confidence and resilience.

As we move further into the digital age, the opportunities for building an online business or influencer brand are virtually endless. With the rise of social media and digital platforms, it's easier than ever to connect with a global audience and share your message with the world. However, the path to online success is not always easy, and requires a great deal of hard work, persistence, and dedication.

The purpose of this book is to provide readers with a comprehensive guide to building a successful and sustainable online business or influencer brand. By exploring the common challenges and roadblocks that individuals face when building an online presence, and providing practical tips and strategies for overcoming these obstacles, readers will be equipped with the tools and knowledge they need to succeed in the digital world.

In the previous sections, we discussed the allure of online success and how it can be deceiving. We explored the pressure to present a perfect image online, the distorted view of success that is based more on appearances than on actual financial or professional success, and the unrealistic expectations that can create a false sense of success.

We also discussed the potential pitfalls and challenges of building an online business or influencer brand. These include generating revenue, staying up-to-date with the latest trends and technologies, and cultivating a strong support network. Additionally, we talked about the pressure to be constantly "on," the sense of isolation and disconnection that can come with working online, and the feelings of imposter syndrome and self-doubt that can arise.

Now, we will dive deeper into these challenges and provide practical advice and strategies for overcoming them. In this section, we will explore the importance of cultivating a strong personal brand, and how to create digital products or services that resonate with your audience.

Building a personal brand is one of the most important steps you can take when building an online business or influencer brand. Your personal brand is a reflection of who you are and what you stand for, and it can help you differentiate yourself from your competitors and establish a unique and recognizable online presence.

To build a strong personal brand, it's important to focus on authenticity and consistency. This means being true to who you are, and consistently delivering on your brand promise in all of your online interactions. Whether you're creating social media posts, publishing blog content, or interacting with your audience on live streams, your personal brand should be evident in everything you do.

Another important aspect of building a successful online business or influencer brand is creating digital products or services that resonate with your audience. This might include eBooks, courses, coaching services, or other digital offerings that provide value to your followers and help them achieve their goals.

When creating digital products or services, it's important to focus on providing real value to your audience. This means identifying their pain points and needs, and creating products or services that address these challenges in a meaningful way. By providing real value to your audience, you can establish trust and credibility, and build a loyal and engaged following.

In addition to creating digital products or services, partnering with brands for sponsored content can be an effective way to monetize your online presence. However, it's important to approach sponsored content partnerships with care and consideration. You should only partner with brands that align with your values and brand message, and ensure that sponsored content is clearly labeled and transparent to your audience.

Overall, building a successful and sustainable online business or influencer brand requires a combination of strategy, creativity, and dedication. By focusing on authenticity, creating value for your audience, and cultivating a strong personal brand, you can establish a unique and recognizable online presence that resonates with your followers and sets you up for long-term success.

The Online Landscape

The online landscape is a vast and ever-changing world, full of endless possibilities and opportunities for growth and success. With the rise of social media, e-commerce, and digital marketing, it's easier than ever to build an online business or influencer brand and connect with a global audience.

However, the online world can also be deceiving. With the constant pressure to present a perfect image, the distorted view of success that is based more on appearances than on actual financial or professional success, and the unrealistic expectations that can create a false sense of success, it's easy to get lost in the online noise and lose sight of what truly matters.

This is why it's important to have a clear understanding of the online landscape, including the challenges and pitfalls that come with building an online business or influencer brand. By understanding the current state of the online world, we can better navigate the challenges and roadblocks that come with online success and build an authentic and sustainable online presence that truly resonates with our audience.

In this chapter, we will explore the current state of the online landscape, including the evolution of the internet, the rise of social media, e-commerce and online marketplaces, digital advertising and marketing, cybersecurity and online safety, and the future of the online world.

By understanding these key trends and technologies, we can begin to build a foundation for success in the digital world. However, it's important to approach the online landscape with caution and skepticism. The allure of online success can be deceiving, and it's easy to get caught up in the hype and lose sight of our true goals and values.

In the following sections, we will explore each of these topics in more detail, and provide practical advice and strategies for navigating the challenges of the online landscape. Whether you're building an online business, launching an influencer brand, or simply looking to establish a strong online presence, this chapter will provide you with the knowledge and tools you need to succeed in the digital world.

But first, let's take a closer look at the evolution of the internet, and how it has transformed the way we communicate, work, and interact with the world around us.

The Evolution of the Internet

The internet has come a long way since its inception in the 1960s. Originally developed as a means of communication between government agencies and universities, it has since evolved into a global network that connects people, businesses, and devices from around the world.

One of the key technological advancements that shaped the internet was the development of the World Wide Web in the late 1980s. This allowed users to access and share information using a standardized protocol, making it easier for people to create and publish content online.

Over the next few decades, the internet continued to evolve, with the introduction of new technologies such as broadband internet, Wi-Fi, and mobile devices. These advancements made it easier for people to connect to the internet from virtually anywhere and paved the way for the rise of social media, e-commerce, and digital marketing.

The rise of social media in particular has had a profound impact on the online landscape. With popular social media platforms, people are able to connect with friends and family, share information and opinions, and build online communities around shared interests and values.

For businesses, social media has become a critical tool for building brand awareness and engaging with customers. Through targeted advertising and strategic content creation, businesses can reach a wider audience and build a loyal customer base.

However, the constant pressure to present a perfect image on social media can also be overwhelming. The rise of "influencer culture" has created a distorted view of success that is based more on appearances than on actual financial or professional success. This can lead to unrealistic expectations and a false sense of success, which can be damaging to both individuals and businesses.

In addition to social media, e-commerce and online marketplaces have also disrupted traditional retail models. With popular e-commerce platforms, people are able to buy and sell products online from anywhere in the world, creating new opportunities for entrepreneurs and small businesses.

Digital advertising and marketing have also become critical tools for building an online presence. Through targeted advertising and strategic content creation, businesses can reach a wider audience and drive conversions. However, the constantly changing landscape of digital marketing can be difficult to navigate, and requires a great deal of knowledge and expertise.

Cybersecurity and online safety have also become increasingly important in today's digital landscape. With the rise of cybercrime and identity theft, it's more important than ever to protect personal and sensitive information online. Best practices for online safety include using strong passwords, avoiding public Wi-Fi networks, and being cautious when sharing personal information online.

As we look to the future of the online landscape, there are many exciting opportunities and challenges ahead. Emerging technologies such as virtual reality and augmented reality have the potential to revolutionize the way we work and interact online. However, it's important to approach these technologies with caution and skepticism, and to be mindful of the potential risks and pitfalls that come with new advancements.

In the following sections of this chapter, we will explore each of these topics in more detail, and provide practical advice and strategies for navigating the challenges and opportunities of the online landscape. By understanding the current state of the online world, we can better position ourselves for success and build an authentic and sustainable online presence that truly resonates with our audience.

The Rise of Social Media

The rise of social media has had a profound impact on the online landscape. With social media platforms, people are able to connect with friends and family, share information and opinions, and build online communities around shared interests and values.

Social media has become an integral part of our daily lives, with billions of people around the world logging on to these platforms each day. From sharing photos and videos, to keeping up with news and trends, social media has transformed the way we communicate and interact with the world around us.

However, the rise of social media has also brought its fair share of challenges and pitfalls. One of the biggest issues with social media is the constant pressure to present a perfect image online. People are bombarded with images of seemingly perfect lives and unrealistic standards of beauty, which can lead to feelings of inadequacy and low self-esteem.

In addition to this, social media has also been blamed for contributing to the spread of fake news and misinformation. The ability to share information quickly and easily has led to the spread of false or misleading information, which can have serious consequences for public health and safety.

For businesses, social media has become a critical tool for building brand awareness and engaging with customers. Through targeted advertising and strategic content creation, businesses can reach a wider audience and build a loyal customer base.

However, the constantly changing landscape of social media can be difficult to navigate. Algorithms change frequently, making it difficult to keep up with the latest trends and best practices. In addition, the sheer volume of content on these platforms can make it difficult for businesses to stand out and get noticed.

Despite these challenges, social media remains a powerful tool for building an online presence and connecting with audiences. By understanding the unique features and strengths of each platform, businesses can create content that resonates with their audience and drives conversions.

Social media has completely transformed the way we interact with one another and consume information. These platforms have become ubiquitous in our daily lives, with billions of users worldwide logging onto these platforms each day.

One of the biggest impacts of social media is its ability to connect people from around the world. Friends and family members who are separated by great distances can stay connected through social media, sharing updates and photos of their daily lives. Social media has also given rise to online communities where people with shared interests and values can come together and connect with one another.

However, the rise of social media has also brought its fair share of challenges and pitfalls. One of the most significant issues with social media is the constant pressure to present a perfect image online. People are bombarded with images of seemingly perfect lives and unrealistic standards of beauty, which can lead to feelings of inadequacy and low self-esteem.

In addition to this, social media has also been blamed for contributing to the spread of fake news and misinformation. The ability to share information quickly and easily has led to the spread of false or misleading information, which can have serious consequences for public health and safety.

For businesses, social media has become a critical tool for building brand awareness and engaging with customers. Through targeted advertising and strategic content creation, businesses can reach a wider audience and build a loyal customer base. Social media also provides businesses with valuable insights into consumer behavior and preferences, allowing them to tailor their marketing strategies accordingly.

However, the constantly changing landscape of social media can be difficult to navigate. Algorithms change frequently, making it difficult to keep up with the latest trends and best practices. In addition, the sheer volume of content on these platforms can make it difficult for businesses to stand out and get noticed.

Despite these challenges, social media remains a powerful tool for building an online presence and connecting with audiences. By understanding the unique features and strengths of each platform, businesses can create content that resonates with their audience and drives conversions.

For example, visual platforms are ideal for showcasing products and services through photos and videos. Short message platforms, on the other hand, is ideal for real-time updates and sharing news and information. Professional networking platform is ideal for building relationships with other businesses and professionals.

By understanding the nuances of each platform, businesses can create a strong and authentic online presence that truly resonates with their audience. This requires staying up-to-date with the latest trends and best practices, as well as developing a deep understanding of the needs and preferences of their target audience.

Overall, the rise of social media has transformed the way we communicate and interact with the world around us. While there are certainly challenges and pitfalls to be aware of, social media remains a powerful tool for building an online presence and connecting with audiences. By staying up-to-date with the latest trends and best practices, businesses and individuals can make the most of the opportunities that social media has to offer.

E-commerce and Online Marketplaces

E-commerce and online marketplaces have revolutionized the way we shop and do business. With e-commerce platforms, people can easily buy and sell products and services from anywhere in the world. This has created a new era of entrepreneurship, where anyone with a good idea and a strong work ethic can start their own online business.

One of the biggest advantages of e-commerce is the ability to reach a wider audience. With an online store, businesses can sell products to customers all over the world, without the need for a physical storefront. This opens up new markets and opportunities for businesses that may not have been possible before.

In addition to this, e-commerce platforms offer a range of tools and services to help businesses build their online presence and reach more customers. From search engine optimization (SEO) to social media marketing, these platforms provide businesses with the resources they need to succeed in the online marketplace.

However, there are also challenges associated with e-commerce and online marketplaces. For example, the competition can be fierce, with thousands of other businesses vying for the same customers. This requires businesses to have a strong understanding of their target audience, as well as the ability to create compelling and engaging content that sets them apart from their competitors.

In addition to this, e-commerce platforms can be complex and challenging to navigate. From setting up an online store to managing inventory and shipping, there are many moving parts to keep track of. This can be overwhelming for new business owners and requires a significant investment of time and resources to get right.

Despite these challenges, e-commerce and online marketplaces offer a wealth of opportunities for entrepreneurs and small business owners. By leveraging the power of these platforms, businesses can reach a wider audience, build brand awareness, and generate revenue in new and exciting ways.

With over 2.5 million active sellers, on one of the most popular shopping application, has become a dominant force in the world of online commerce. The platform offers a range of tools and services to help sellers build their online presence, including product listings, advertising, and fulfillment services.

Another popular e-commerce platform is eBay. Founded in 1995, eBay has grown to become one of the largest online marketplaces in the world. The platform allows sellers to list and sell products in a wide range of categories, from fashion and electronics to home goods and collectibles.

Etsy is another popular platform that has gained popularity in recent years. Founded in 2005, Etsy is a marketplace that specializes in handmade and vintage goods. The platform has a strong community of sellers and buyers, and offers a range of tools and services to help sellers build their online presence and connect with customers.

In addition to these platforms, there are also a range of other e-commerce tools and services available to businesses. From Shopify to WooCommerce, there are a wealth of options for businesses looking to build their online presence and reach more customer.

One of the most important factors in building a successful online business is search engine optimization (SEO). SEO is the process of optimizing your website and content to rank higher in search engine results pages (SERPs), which can drive more traffic to your site and increase your visibility online.

While SEO can be a powerful tool for driving organic traffic to your website, it can also be complex and challenging to navigate. Search engine algorithms are constantly changing, which means that businesses must stay up-to-date with the latest trends and best practices in order to stay ahead of the competition.

In addition to this, there are many different factors that go into optimizing your website and content for search engines. From keyword research and on-page optimization to link building and content creation, there are many moving parts to keep track of.

For businesses that are just starting out, SEO can be overwhelming and challenging to navigate. This requires a significant investment of time and resources in order to get right, and may require the help of a professional SEO consultant or agency.

Despite these challenges, SEO remains a critical component of any successful online business strategy. By optimizing your website and content for search engines, businesses can drive more organic traffic to their site, increase their visibility online, and ultimately generate more leads and revenue.

Overall, the online landscape is complex and constantly changing. From social media and e-commerce platforms to search engine optimization and content marketing, there are many different factors to consider when building an online business or influencer brand. By staying up-to-date with the latest trends and best practices, businesses and individuals can make the most of the opportunities that the online landscape has to offer.

Digital Advertising and Marketing

Digital advertising and marketing have become an essential component of any successful online business or influencer brand. With billions of people using social media and other online platforms every day, businesses and individuals have the ability to reach a wider audience than ever before.

However, digital advertising and marketing can also be challenging and complex. With so many different platforms and channels to choose from, it can be difficult to know where to focus your efforts and which strategies will be most effective.

One of the biggest challenges in digital advertising and marketing is the competition. With so many businesses and individuals vying for the attention of consumers, it can be difficult to stand out from the crowd. This requires a strong understanding of your target audience, as well as the ability to create compelling and engaging content that resonates with them.

In addition to this, digital advertising and marketing require a significant investment of time and resources. From creating content to managing social media accounts and running ad campaigns, there are many moving parts to keep track of. This can be overwhelming for businesses and individuals, especially those who are just starting out.

Another challenge in digital advertising and marketing is the constantly changing landscape. Social media algorithms are constantly evolving, which means that businesses and individuals must stay up-to-date with the latest trends and best practices in order to be successful.

Despite these challenges, digital advertising and marketing offer a wealth of opportunities for businesses and individuals. By leveraging the power of social media and other online platforms, businesses can reach a wider audience, build brand awareness, and generate revenue in new and exciting ways.

One of the most popular digital advertising platforms is a social media platform Ads. With over 2.8 billion monthly active users, it offers a powerful advertising platform that allows businesses to target specific audiences and reach a wider audience. The platform offers a range of tools and services to help businesses create and run effective ad campaigns, including detailed targeting options and analytics.

Another popular platform is the most popular search engine's Ads. With over 5 billion daily searches, Ads offers a powerful advertising platform that allows businesses to reach customers who are actively searching for their products or services. The platform offers a range of targeting options, including keywords, demographics, and location.

In addition to these platforms, there are a range of other digital advertising and marketing tools and services available to businesses and individuals. From influencer marketing to email marketing and content marketing, there are many different strategies and tactics that businesses can use to reach their target audience and build their online presence.

Overall, digital advertising and marketing offer a range of opportunities for businesses and individuals looking to build their online presence and generate revenue. While there are certainly challenges to be aware of, the potential for growth and success in the online landscape is significant. By staying up-to-date with the latest trends and best practices, businesses and individuals can make the most of the opportunities that digital advertising and marketing have to offer.

Freelancing

Freelancing has become an increasingly popular option for individuals looking to build an online business or influencer brand. With the ability to work from anywhere and set their own schedules, freelancers have the freedom and flexibility to pursue their passions and build their careers on their own terms.

However, freelancing also comes with a number of challenges. One of the biggest challenges is finding consistent work. With so many freelancers competing for jobs, it can be difficult to stand out from the crowd and secure regular clients. This requires a strong understanding of your target audience, as well as the ability to create compelling and engaging proposals and pitches that set you apart from other freelancers.

Another challenge in freelancing is managing your workload and time effectively. With no set schedule or supervisor, it can be easy to become overwhelmed or distracted, leading to missed deadlines and dissatisfied clients. This requires a strong sense of self-discipline and time-management skills, as well as the ability to set realistic goals and priorities.

In addition to these challenges, freelancers also have to manage their own finances and taxes, which can be confusing and overwhelming for those who are not familiar with the process. This requires a strong understanding of tax laws and regulations, as well as the ability to track income and expenses effectively.

Despite these challenges, freelancing offers a number of benefits for individuals looking to build their careers online. By leveraging their skills and expertise, freelancers can offer a range of services and solutions to clients around the world, from writing and design to marketing and programming.

With over 3 million active buyers, one of the most popular freelance marketplaces offers a powerful platform that allows freelancers to connect with clients and offer their services. The platform offers a range of tools and services to help freelancers market themselves effectively and build their online presence.

With over 12 million registered freelancers and 5 million registered clients, another marketplace offers a powerful platform for freelancers to connect with clients and find work. The platform offers a range of tools and services to help freelancers build their profiles and showcase their skills and experience.

In addition to these platforms, there are a range of other freelancing opportunities available to individuals looking to build their careers online. From freelance writing and graphic design to web development and programming, there are many different skills and services that can be leveraged to build a successful freelancing business.

Overall, freelancing offers a wealth of opportunities for individuals looking to build their careers online. While there are certainly challenges to be aware of, the potential for growth and success is significant. By staying up-to-date with the latest trends and best practices, freelancers can make the most of the opportunities that freelancing has to offer.

Cybersecurity and Online Safety

In today's increasingly interconnected world, cybersecurity and online safety have become essential components of any successful online business or influencer brand. With the vast amount of sensitive and personal information being shared online, it's more important than ever to take proactive steps to protect yourself and your business from cyber threats and attacks.

One of the biggest challenges in cybersecurity and online safety is the constantly evolving nature of cyber threats. Hackers and cybercriminals are constantly developing new tactics and techniques to gain access to sensitive information, which means that individuals and businesses must stay up-to-date with the latest security measures and best practices to stay protected.

Another challenge in cybersecurity and online safety is the human element. While technology can help protect against cyber threats, it's often the actions of individuals that can lead to security breaches. This includes things like weak passwords, phishing scams, and social engineering attacks.

To mitigate these risks, it's important to take a multi-layered approach to cybersecurity and online safety. This includes a combination of technological solutions, such as antivirus software, firewalls, and intrusion detection systems, as well as best practices and policies aimed at reducing the risk of human error.

One of the most effective ways to reduce the risk of cyber threats and attacks is to establish a culture of cybersecurity within your business or influencer brand. This can involve regular training and education for employees and team members on how to recognize and prevent cyber threats, as well as clear policies and guidelines on data security and privacy.

In addition to establishing a culture of cybersecurity, there are a range of tools and services available to help individuals and businesses stay protected online. This includes security consulting and training services, as well as online tools and services for data encryption and secure communication.

Another challenge in cybersecurity and online safety is the increasing prevalence of cybercrime and cyberattacks. In recent years, there has been a significant increase in the number of data breaches and cyberattacks, with cybercriminals targeting everything from small businesses to large corporations.

To protect against these risks, it's important to be proactive in identifying and mitigating potential threats. This may involve conducting regular security audits and risk assessments, as well as establishing clear incident response plans in the event of a cyberattack or data breach.

Overall, cybersecurity and online safety are essential components of any successful online business or influencer brand. While there are certainly challenges to be aware of, the potential consequences of cyber threats and attacks make it essential to take proactive steps to protect yourself and your business. By staying up-to-date with the latest security measures and best practices, individuals and businesses can minimize their risk and stay protected in today's digital landscape.

The Future of the Online Landscape

The future of the online landscape is a constantly evolving and dynamic environment, with new challenges and opportunities emerging on a regular basis. From the growing importance of data privacy and security to the rise of new technologies and business models, there are a number of factors that are shaping the future of online business and influencer brands.

One of the key challenges facing the online landscape is the increasing importance of data privacy and security. With the rise of new data privacy regulations, such as the GDPR and the California Consumer Privacy Act, businesses and influencers are under increasing pressure to ensure that they are protecting the privacy and security of their users' data. This requires a comprehensive approach to data privacy and security, including regular audits, risk assessments, and employee training.

Another challenge facing the online landscape is the growing importance of artificial intelligence and machine learning. As these technologies continue to advance, they are expected to have a significant impact on the online landscape, particularly in areas such as e-commerce, marketing, and customer service. This requires businesses and influencers to stay up-to-date with the latest developments in AI and machine learning, and to develop strategies for incorporating these technologies into their online operations.

At the same time, there are a number of new technologies and platforms emerging that are changing the way that businesses and influencers engage with their audiences. For example, virtual and augmented reality technologies are allowing businesses to create immersive online experiences, while blockchain and cryptocurrency technologies are providing new ways of transacting online. These technologies have the potential to transform the online landscape in the years to come, creating new opportunities for innovation and growth.

Despite these challenges, there are also a number of opportunities emerging in the online landscape. As more and more businesses and influencers move online, there is a growing demand for digital skills and expertise, particularly in areas such as web development, online marketing, and social media management. This requires businesses and influencers to invest in the development of these skills, either through training or by hiring experienced professionals.

In addition to these opportunities, there are also a number of new business models emerging in the online landscape. For example, the sharing economy and the gig economy are providing new ways of working and engaging with customers, while subscription-based models are changing the way that businesses monetize their online content. These business models have the potential to create new opportunities for growth and innovation in the online landscape.

Overall, the future of the online landscape is both exciting and challenging. As new technologies and platforms emerge, businesses and influencers must stay up-to-date with the latest trends and best practices in order to succeed in this rapidly evolving environment. By taking a proactive approach to data privacy and security, staying on top of emerging trends and technologies, and embracing new business models and opportunities, businesses and influencers can position themselves for success in the years to come.

As we've explored in this chapter, the online landscape is a constantly evolving and dynamic environment that is both challenging and exciting. It offers endless possibilities for businesses and influencers to reach new audiences, connect with customers, and build their brands.

One of the key takeaways from this chapter is the importance of understanding the challenges and opportunities of the online landscape. From data privacy and security to emerging technologies and business models, there are a number of factors that are shaping the future of online business and influencer brands.

One of the biggest challenges facing the online landscape is the need to balance the benefits of online engagement with the risks of data privacy and security. As we've seen, the rise of new data privacy regulations and the growing importance of artificial intelligence and machine learning have created significant challenges for businesses and influencers. However, by taking a proactive approach to data privacy and security, businesses and influencers can protect their users' data and build trust with their audiences.

Another key challenge facing the online landscape is the need to stay up-to-date with emerging trends and technologies. With new platforms and technologies emerging all the time, it can be difficult for businesses and influencers to keep pace. However, by investing in the development of digital skills and expertise, staying on top of emerging trends, and embracing new business models and opportunities, businesses and influencers can position themselves for success in the years to come.

Despite these challenges, the online landscape offers significant opportunities for growth and innovation. As more and more businesses and influencers move online, there is a growing demand for digital skills and expertise, particularly in areas such as web development, online marketing, and social media management. This presents an opportunity for businesses and influencers to develop new skills and expand their reach.

In addition to these opportunities, there are also a number of new business models emerging in the online landscape. For example, the sharing economy and the gig economy are providing new ways of working and engaging with customers, while subscription-based models are changing the way that businesses monetize their online content. These business models have the potential to create new opportunities for growth and innovation in the online landscape.

Overall, the online landscape is a complex and challenging environment, but one that offers significant opportunities for growth and innovation. By understanding the challenges and opportunities of this environment, businesses and influencers can position themselves for success in the years to come.

The Dark Side of Social Media

The rise of social media has transformed the way we interact with each other and the world around us. Social media platforms have become a ubiquitous part of modern life, with billions of people logging on every day to share their thoughts, feelings, and experiences with others.

While social media has undoubtedly brought about many positive changes, such as enabling us to connect with people all over the world, it has also had a profound impact on society. In this chapter, we will explore the darker side of social media and the impact that it is having on our lives.

At its core, social media is about connection and community. It enables us to communicate with others in ways that were once unimaginable, bridging distances and bringing people together in new and exciting ways. Whether we are sharing photos of our latest vacation or discussing the latest news and trends, social media has become an integral part of our daily lives.

However, this unprecedented level of connectivity has also given rise to new challenges and risks. One of the most significant of these is the impact of social media on our mental health. Studies have shown that social media use is linked to an increased risk of anxiety and depression, as well as other mental health issues such as low self-esteem and body image issues.

Furthermore, social media has also become a breeding ground for the spread of misinformation, fake news, and propaganda. With the ability to share information quickly and easily, social media has become a powerful tool for those looking to spread false information and manipulate public opinion.

In addition to these risks, social media has also become a platform for cyberbullying and online harassment. The anonymity and distance provided by social media have made it easier than ever for people to engage in abusive and harassing behavior, often with little to no consequences.

Finally, social media has also become a tool for the manipulation of politics and society. From the spread of propaganda to the use of social media to influence public opinion and election outcomes, social media has become a powerful tool for those looking to manipulate the political and social landscape.

Social media has become an integral part of our lives, connecting us with friends, family, and the world around us. These social media platforms have transformed the way we communicate and interact with each other. However, there is a darker side to social media that is often overlooked.

While we may view social media as a positive force in our lives, the truth is that it can also have a significant negative impact. From cyberbullying and online harassment to the spread of misinformation and fake news, social media has become a breeding ground for some of the worst aspects of human behavior.

One of the biggest issues with social media is the impact that it can have on our mental health. Studies have shown that social media use can lead to feelings of anxiety, depression, and loneliness, as well as other mental health issues such as low self-esteem and body image issues. Social media can also be highly addictive, with many people spending hours every day scrolling through their feeds, checking notifications, and seeking validation from others.

Another significant issue with social media is the spread of misinformation and fake news. With the ability to share information quickly and easily, social media has become a powerful tool for those looking to spread false information and manipulate public opinion. This can have serious consequences, such as the spread of conspiracy theories, the erosion of trust in institutions, and even the potential for violence.

Cyberbullying and online harassment are also significant problems on social media. The anonymity and distance provided by these platforms make it easier than ever for people to engage in abusive and harassing behavior, often with little to no consequences. This can have a devastating impact on the mental health and well-being of those targeted, and it can also have broader societal implications, such as the normalization of abusive behavior.

Finally, social media has become a tool for the manipulation of politics and society. From the spread of propaganda to the use of social media to influence public opinion and election outcomes, social media has become a powerful tool for those looking to manipulate the political and social landscape.

In this chapter, we will explore each of these topics in more detail, providing an in-depth analysis of the darker side of social media and the impact that it is having on our lives. By understanding these risks, we can take steps to protect ourselves and others from the negative effects of social media and work towards building a more positive and constructive online landscape.

The Psychological Effects of Social Media

Social media has become an integral part of our lives, and for many of us, it has become a constant companion. From the moment we wake up to the moment we go to bed, we are bombarded with information, images, and updates from our social media feeds. While there are certainly benefits to this level of connectivity, there are also significant psychological effects that are often overlooked.

One of the most significant psychological effects of social media is the impact that it can have on our self-esteem and body image. With the constant stream of images and updates from our social media feeds, it is easy to compare ourselves to others and feel inadequate. This can lead to feelings of anxiety, depression, and low self-esteem, as well as more serious mental health issues such as eating disorders and body dysmorphia.

Another psychological effect of social media is the impact that it can have on our attention span and ability to focus. With so much information competing for our attention, it can be difficult to concentrate on any one thing for an extended period. This can lead to a sense of overwhelm and burnout, as well as a decrease in productivity and creativity.

Social media can also have a profound impact on our relationships and social interactions. While it is certainly true that social media can help us connect with people all over the world, it can also create a sense of isolation and disconnection. Many people report feeling more lonely and disconnected from others despite being more connected than ever before.

Another psychological effect of social media is the impact that it can have on our emotional regulation. With so much negativity and drama on social media, it can be easy to become emotionally overwhelmed and reactive. This can lead to a cycle of stress and anxiety that can be difficult to break.

In addition to these psychological effects, social media can also have a significant impact on our physical health. With so much screen time and sedentary behavior, social media use has been linked to a number of physical health issues, including obesity, poor sleep, and eye strain.

Impact of social media on self-esteem and body image:

The impact of social media on self-esteem and body image is a complex and multifaceted issue. On one hand, social media can provide a platform for positive body image messages, and can even be a source of support and inspiration for those struggling with body image issues. On the other hand, social media can also contribute to negative body image and self-esteem, particularly for those who are already vulnerable to these issues.

One of the main ways in which social media can impact self-esteem and body image is through the constant stream of images and updates from our feeds. With so many images of "perfect" bodies and idealized lifestyles, it is easy to compare ourselves to others and feel inadequate. This can lead to feelings of anxiety, depression, and low self-esteem, as well as more serious mental health issues such as eating disorders and body dysmorphia.

Another way in which social media can impact self-esteem and body image is through the use of filters and editing tools. With the ability to retouch and alter images, social media can create an unrealistic and unattainable standard of beauty that can be damaging to those who do not fit this mold. This can lead to feelings of inadequacy and low self-esteem, as well as a distorted view of what is "normal" or "acceptable" when it comes to appearance.

The impact of social media on self-esteem and body image is particularly acute for young people, who are often more susceptible to these messages and may lack the emotional and psychological maturity to navigate them effectively. Research has shown that young people who spend more time on social media are more likely to report negative body image and self-esteem, as well as a greater likelihood of engaging in unhealthy weight control behaviors.

It is important to note that social media can also be a source of support and inspiration for those struggling with body image issues. With the rise of body positivity movements and the increasing visibility of diverse body types and sizes on social media, there is a growing sense of acceptance and inclusivity that can be empowering for those who have felt marginalized or excluded in the past.

However, it is clear that the impact of social media on self-esteem and body image is a complex and nuanced issue, with both positive and negative aspects. By being aware of the potential risks and challenges associated with social media use, we can take steps to protect our mental health and work towards building a more positive and constructive online landscape.

The addictive nature of social media and its impact on our lives:

Social media has become an integral part of modern life, and for many people, it is an essential tool for staying connected with friends and family, as well as for work and personal development. However, the addictive nature of social media has become a growing concern, with many experts warning about the potential negative impact on our lives.

One of the main reasons that social media can be so addictive is the way it is designed. Social media platforms are designed to be engaging, with features such as likes, comments, and shares that provide instant gratification and a sense of social validation. This can create a powerful incentive to keep checking our feeds and interacting with others online, even when we know it is not necessarily the best use of our time.

The addictive nature of social media can also be reinforced by the social pressure to be constantly connected and up-to-date with the latest news and trends. Many people feel a sense of FOMO (fear of missing out) if they are not constantly checking their feeds, and this can create a sense of anxiety and stress that can be difficult to shake.

The impact of social media addiction can be far-reaching, affecting everything from our mental health and well-being to our relationships and productivity. Research has shown that social media addiction can lead to increased feelings of anxiety, depression, and loneliness, as well as decreased levels of happiness and life satisfaction. It can also contribute to sleep problems, reduced productivity, and even physical health issues such as headaches and eye strain.

One of the biggest challenges with social media addiction is that it can be difficult to recognize and address. Many people are unaware of the extent to which social media is impacting their lives, and may not even realize that they have a problem until it is too late. This is why it is so important to be aware of the potential risks and challenges associated with social media use, and to take steps to manage our online habits in a healthy and constructive way.

Overall, the addictive nature of social media is a growing concern, and one that requires careful attention and consideration. By understanding the impact of social media addiction on our lives and taking steps to manage our use of these platforms, we can work towards building a more positive and balanced relationship with technology.

The Spread of Misinformation

Social media has become a powerful tool for spreading information and ideas, but unfortunately, it has also become a breeding ground for misinformation and propaganda. The spread of misinformation on social media can have serious consequences, from fueling political polarization to undermining public health and safety.

One of the main reasons that social media is so effective at spreading misinformation is its ability to amplify certain messages and drown out others. Social media algorithms are designed to prioritize content that is likely to engage users, regardless of its accuracy or relevance. This means that sensational or controversial content often rises to the top of our feeds, while more factual or nuanced information may be buried or ignored.

Another factor contributing to the spread of misinformation on social media is the ease with which it can be shared and disseminated. With just a few clicks, a misleading or false story can be shared with thousands or even millions of people, potentially creating significant harm in the process.

The consequences of misinformation on social media can be far-reaching and wide-ranging. In the political sphere, misinformation can contribute to political polarization and fuel the spread of conspiracy theories and extremist ideologies. In the realm of public health, misinformation can lead to dangerous and even deadly outcomes, such as the spread of anti-vaccine sentiment or the promotion of unproven or harmful treatments for serious medical conditions.

Addressing the spread of misinformation on social media requires a multifaceted approach that involves a combination of technological solutions, regulatory measures, and individual responsibility. Social media companies can work to improve their algorithms to prioritize accurate and reliable information, while governments can establish regulations to combat the spread of false or misleading content online. At the individual level, we can all work to become more discerning consumers of information, taking the time to fact-check and verify the information we encounter online before sharing it with others.

The spread of misinformation on social media has become a significant concern in recent years, with numerous examples of the harm it can cause. One notable recent example is the spread of false information related to the COVID-19 pandemic, which has had serious implications for public health and safety.

In the early stages of the pandemic, for example, false information about the virus and its origins was widely circulated on social media. This included conspiracy theories that the virus was artificially created in a lab, as well as misinformation about its transmission and prevention. These false claims led to confusion and panic among the public, as well as a lack of trust in public health officials and scientific experts.

Another example of the spread of misinformation on social media is the phenomenon of "fake news," which has been a concern since the 2016 U.S. presidential election. During the election, false stories and conspiracy theories were circulated on social media, with some suggesting that they may have influenced the outcome of the election. Since then, the problem of fake news has only continued to grow, with false stories and propaganda being used to manipulate public opinion on a wide range of issues.

The consequences of the spread of misinformation on social media can be profound. In addition to undermining public trust in institutions and experts, it can also have serious implications for public health and safety. For example, false information about the COVID-19 pandemic has led to individuals refusing to wear masks or get vaccinated, which has contributed to the continued spread of the virus.

As social media continues to play an increasingly prominent role in our lives, it is more important than ever to be vigilant about the information we encounter online. By taking the time to fact-check and verify information before sharing it with others, we can help to combat the spread of misinformation and ensure that social media remains a positive force in our world.

Overall, the spread of misinformation on social media is a serious and growing problem, one that requires careful attention and action from all stakeholders. By working together to combat the spread of false or misleading information, we can help to ensure that social media remains a force for good in the world.

The impact of fake news on politics and society:

The phenomenon of "fake news" has become an increasingly prevalent issue in recent years, with serious implications for politics and society. The spread of false information through social media and other online platforms has created a landscape in which it can be difficult to discern truth from fiction, leading to confusion and a lack of trust in traditional news sources.

One of the most significant impacts of fake news on politics is its potential to manipulate public opinion and influence election outcomes. By spreading false stories and propaganda, individuals or groups with a particular agenda can sway public opinion in their favor, potentially leading to a skewed electoral result. This was evident in the 2016 U.S. presidential election, in which fake news stories were circulated on social media in an attempt to influence voter behavior.

The impact of fake news on society goes beyond the realm of politics, however. It can also contribute to the spread of harmful and dangerous ideas, such as conspiracy theories or hate speech. For example, false information about the COVID-19 pandemic has led to individuals refusing to wear masks or get vaccinated, which has contributed to the continued spread of the virus. False information about social issues such as race and gender can also contribute to the perpetuation of harmful stereotypes and discrimination.

Combatting the spread of fake news is a complex and multifaceted issue. It requires a combination of efforts from social media companies, traditional news sources, and individuals. Social media companies can work to improve their algorithms to prioritize accurate and reliable information, while traditional news sources can work to rebuild trust with their audiences by emphasizing the importance of accurate reporting. At the individual level, we can all work to become more discerning consumers of information, fact-checking and verifying the sources of the information we encounter online.

Overall, the impact of fake news on politics and society is a serious concern that requires careful attention and action from all stakeholders. By working together to combat the spread of false information, we can help to ensure that our society remains grounded in truth and accuracy, rather than misinformation and propaganda.

Cyberbullying and Online Harassment:

Cyberbullying and online harassment have become increasingly prevalent in today's world. With the rise of social media, it has become easier for people to bully and harass others from behind the safety of their screens. This section will explore the various forms of cyberbullying and online harassment, as well as their impact on victims.

One of the most common forms of cyberbullying is harassment on social media platforms. This can take the form of targeted comments, messages, or posts designed to humiliate or intimidate the victim. In some cases, the harassment can be ongoing, with the victim receiving multiple messages or comments over a period of time.

Another form of cyberbullying is the use of fake accounts or anonymous profiles to harass others. This can make it difficult for victims to identify their harassers, and can also make it more difficult for law enforcement to take action against them.

The impact of cyberbullying and online harassment can be severe. Victims often experience anxiety, depression, and other mental health issues as a result of the harassment. They may also experience physical symptoms such as headaches or stomachaches, and may have difficulty sleeping or eating.

In some cases, cyberbullying and online harassment can also have long-term consequences. Victims may find it difficult to trust others or to form new relationships, and may also experience difficulty in school

41

or at work. In extreme cases, cyberbullying and online harassment can even lead to suicide.

Despite the prevalence of cyberbullying and online harassment, it can be difficult for victims to seek help or support. Many victims are reluctant to come forward out of fear of further harassment or retaliation, or because they believe that nothing can be done to stop it.

However, there are steps that can be taken to combat cyberbullying and online harassment. Social media platforms can take a more active role in monitoring and removing harassing content, and law enforcement can take action against those who engage in this behavior. In addition, individuals can take steps to protect themselves, such as blocking or reporting harassing accounts, or limiting their social media use.

Overall, cyberbullying and online harassment are serious issues that can have devastating consequences for victims. By raising awareness of these issues and taking steps to combat them, we can work towards creating a safer and more compassionate online environment.

Behind the Façade: Sophie's story

Sophie had always been the life of the party. She loved being the center of attention and was never one to shy away from a challenge. But beneath her confident exterior lay a deep sense of insecurity that she had been carrying with her for as long as she could remember.

As a child, Sophie had been teased mercilessly by her classmates for being overweight. She had spent years trying to lose the extra pounds, but no matter how hard she tried, she could never seem to shed them. The constant teasing had taken its toll on her self-esteem, and she had always felt like an outsider.

Despite her insecurities, Sophie had managed to make a name for herself in the world of social media. She had amassed a huge following on social media, where she shared her daily life with her fans. She loved the attention and validation that came with having so many followers, and she was always looking for ways to increase her online presence.

But as her following grew, so did the pressure to maintain her image. Sophie was constantly worried about what her fans thought of her, and she spent hours every day obsessing over her posts and comments. She became increasingly isolated, spending more and more time online and less time with her friends and family.

One day, Sophie received a message from a fan who claimed to be a modeling scout. The scout told Sophie that she had the perfect look for a new campaign that they were working on and invited her to come to New York for a photoshoot. Sophie was thrilled at the opportunity and immediately agreed to go.

But when she arrived in New York, things quickly took a dark turn. The supposed modeling scout turned out to be a predator who had been preying on young women for years. He drugged Sophie and took explicit photos of her, which he threatened to release if she didn't comply with his demands.

Sophie was terrified. She didn't know who to turn to for help, and she felt like her entire world was crashing down around her. She tried to keep up appearances on social media, but she knew that she couldn't keep the facade up forever.

As the weeks went by, Sophie became increasingly withdrawn. She stopped posting on social media altogether and cut off contact with her friends and family. She felt like she had lost everything that mattered to her, and she didn't know how to move forward.

It wasn't until a chance encounter with a stranger that Sophie began to see a glimmer of hope. The stranger, who had also been a victim of online harassment, told Sophie about a support group for survivors of cyberbullying and online abuse. Sophie was hesitant at first, but she decided to give it a try.

The support group was a turning point for Sophie. She finally felt like she wasn't alone, and she began to open up about her experiences. She learned coping mechanisms for dealing with the trauma she had suffered and found a sense of community among the other survivors.

Sophie's journey was far from over, but she finally felt like she had a path forward. She began to use her platform for good, speaking out about the dangers of online abuse and advocating for other survivors. While she would never forget the trauma that she had endured, she knew that she could use her experience to make a difference in the world.

Addressing Cyberbullying and Online Harassment:

As cyberbullying and online harassment continue to be a growing concern, social media companies are taking measures to address these issues. Companies have implemented various policies and tools to combat cyberbullying and online harassment on their platforms.

One such tool is the ability to report inappropriate content or behavior. Users can report any content that they feel violates community guidelines or is harmful in any way. Social media companies have dedicated teams to review such reports and take action against the perpetrators.

Additionally, social media companies have implemented features such as blocking and muting to help users protect themselves from online harassment. Users can block or mute anyone who they feel is behaving inappropriately towards them, preventing them from seeing or interacting with their content.

Some companies have also implemented artificial intelligence (AI) technology to detect and remove harmful content automatically. This technology uses algorithms to analyze content and flag anything that could be considered harmful or offensive. While AI technology is not perfect and can sometimes flag innocent content, it is a step towards creating a safer online environment.

Despite these measures, cyberbullying and online harassment still persist on social media platforms. Social media companies need to continue to improve their policies and tools to address these issues and create a safer online environment for all users.

Privacy Concerns:

As more and more of our lives move online, privacy concerns have become a major issue. From social media companies collecting and selling our data to hackers stealing our personal information, online privacy is under threat like never before.

In this section, we will delve into the various privacy concerns that arise from using social media and other online services. We will explore the ways in which our data is collected and used, as well as the potential consequences of this data being in the wrong hands.

We will also discuss the measures that can be taken to protect our online privacy and the steps that social media companies are taking to address these concerns. With the increasing importance of online privacy in our daily lives, it is crucial that we understand the risks and take steps to protect ourselves.

Social media has become an integral part of our daily lives. We use it to connect with friends and family, stay up-to-date with news and current events, and even conduct business. However, with the convenience and connectivity that social media provides comes a significant risk to our privacy.

One of the primary privacy risks associated with social media use is the collection and use of our personal data. Social media companies collect vast amounts of data on their users, including our names, ages, locations, and interests. They also collect data on our online behavior, such as the content we interact with and the people we communicate with.

This data is then used for various purposes, including targeted advertising, content recommendation algorithms, and even political campaigning. However, the collection and use of this data also presents significant privacy risks. Hackers and other malicious actors can potentially access this data and use it for nefarious purposes, such as identity theft, fraud, and even blackmail.

Another privacy risk associated with social media use is the potential for cyberstalking and online harassment. Personal information and location data shared on social media can be used to track and target individuals, putting them at risk of stalking and harassment.

Additionally, social media companies have faced criticism for their lack of transparency when it comes to data collection and privacy policies. Many users are unaware of the extent to which their data is being collected and used, and social media companies have faced backlash for their failure to adequately inform users of these practices.

To address these privacy concerns, social media companies have implemented various privacy policies and settings. Users can choose to limit the information they share on social media and adjust their privacy settings to control who can access their data. Social media companies have also faced increasing pressure from regulators to improve their privacy policies and practices.

However, despite these efforts, privacy risks associated with social media use remain a significant concern. Users must remain vigilant and take steps to protect their online privacy, such as being mindful of the information they share and regularly reviewing their privacy settings.

Social Media Data Collection and Use

Social media companies have access to vast amounts of personal data that users willingly provide, such as names, ages, locations, and interests. However, social media companies also collect data on our online behavior, such as the content we interact with and the people we communicate with. This data is used to create detailed user profiles, which are then used for various purposes, including targeted advertising, content recommendation algorithms, and even political campaigning.

One of the primary ways that social media companies collect user data is through tracking. Social media platforms use tracking technologies such as cookies, pixel tags, and web beacons to collect data on users' online behavior. These technologies can track users across different websites and platforms, allowing social media companies to build a more comprehensive profile of users' interests and behaviors.

Social media companies also collect data through user-generated content, such as posts, comments, and likes. This data provides insights into users' opinions and preferences, which can be used to inform advertising and content recommendations.

The collection and use of this data have become increasingly sophisticated, with social media companies using artificial intelligence and machine learning algorithms to analyze user data and make predictions about user behavior. For example, social media companies can use data on users' interests and behavior to predict which advertisements they are most likely to click on or which content they are most likely to engage with.

However, the collection and use of personal data by social media companies have raised significant privacy concerns. Users may be unaware of the extent to which their data is being collected and used, and social media companies have faced criticism for their lack of transparency and inadequate privacy policies.

To address these concerns, social media companies have implemented various privacy policies and settings that allow users to control the information they share and limit the use of their personal data. However, users must remain vigilant and take steps to protect their online privacy, such as regularly reviewing their privacy settings and being mindful of the information they share online.

The impact of data breaches on our personal information and security:

The collection and use of personal data by social media companies come with significant risks, one of which is the potential for data breaches. Data breaches occur when unauthorized individuals gain access to personal data, including names, addresses, phone numbers, email addresses, and even financial information.

Data breaches can have significant consequences for individuals, including identity theft, financial fraud, and damage to personal reputation. In recent years, social media companies have experienced several high-profile data breaches, exposing the personal information of millions of users.

In 2018, one social media platform faced a massive data breach that affected up to 50 million users. The breach was caused by a vulnerability in It's code that allowed hackers to access users' access tokens, which are used to keep users logged in to the platform. This breach allowed hackers to access users' personal data, including their names, email addresses, and phone numbers.

Similarly, in 2019, a data breach at the social media company, it exposed the personal information of over 4.6 million users, including names, phone numbers, and usernames. This breach occurred after a hacker gained access to it's database through a vulnerability in the platform's third-party integration.

The impact of these data breaches can be devastating for individuals, leaving them vulnerable to identity theft and other forms of cybercrime. In response, social media companies have increased their efforts to improve data security and protect users' personal information.

However, despite these efforts, data breaches remain a significant risk for social media users. To protect themselves, users must take steps to secure their personal information, such as creating strong passwords, enabling two-factor authentication, and regularly reviewing their privacy settings.

Protecting Online Privacy and Safeguarding Personal Information:

With the increasing use of social media and online platforms, protecting personal information and online privacy has become more important than ever. Social media companies collect a significant amount of data from users, including personal information such as names, phone numbers, email addresses, and even credit card information. However, there are steps that users can take to safeguard their personal information and protect their online privacy.

1. Review and adjust privacy settings: Users should regularly review their privacy settings on social media platforms and adjust them according to their preferences. For example, users can choose to limit who can see their posts and profile information, as well as control who can send them friend requests.

2. Use strong passwords: Strong passwords can go a long way in protecting online accounts from potential threats. Users should choose unique and complex passwords that are difficult to guess or hack. It is also recommended to use two-factor authentication for added security.

3. Be wary of phishing scams: Phishing scams are common on social media and email. Users should be cautious of suspicious links or emails from unknown sources, as they may contain malware or attempt to steal personal information.

4. Avoid oversharing: Users should be mindful of the information they share online, especially sensitive information such as home addresses, phone numbers, and financial information. Oversharing can leave users vulnerable to identity theft and other forms of cybercrime.

5. Limit app permissions: Users should carefully review the permissions that apps request when downloading and using them. Some apps may ask for access to personal data, such as contacts or location, which may not be necessary for the app's function.

By following these steps, users can take control of their online privacy and safeguard their personal information from potential threats. However, it is important to note that protecting online privacy is an ongoing process and requires constant vigilance and awareness.

In conclusion, social media and online platforms have brought about significant changes in the way we communicate, share information, and conduct business. However, these changes have also brought about a darker side of social media that often goes overlooked. From cyberbullying and online harassment to privacy concerns and data breaches, the risks associated with social media use are numerous and can have serious consequences.

While social media companies are taking steps to address these issues, it is ultimately up to individual users to take responsibility for their online privacy and security. By reviewing and adjusting privacy settings, using strong passwords, being wary of phishing scams, avoiding oversharing, and limiting app permissions, users can take steps to protect their personal information and safeguard their online privacy.

It is important to recognize that protecting online privacy is an ongoing process that requires constant vigilance and awareness. By staying informed and taking proactive measures to protect personal information, users can enjoy the benefits of social media while minimizing the risks associated with its use.

The Illusion of Online Success

As we continue to explore the online landscape and the various issues that come along with it, it is important to recognize that the internet and social media have created a world where success is often measured in likes, followers, and views. The illusion of online success is not only unrealistic, but it can also be unattainable for many individuals who are seeking to establish themselves online.

At the heart of this illusion lies the idea that anyone can become an overnight success. Social media platforms have created an environment where viral videos, memes, and trending hashtags can propel someone to internet fame in a matter of hours. While this kind of rapid success can be exciting, it is also incredibly rare. For most people, building a successful online presence requires years of hard work, dedication, and patience.

The pressure to succeed online can be overwhelming, and the constant comparison to others can be damaging to one's mental health. In the pursuit of online success, individuals often sacrifice their personal relationships, well-being, and even their own values in order to keep up with the competition.

Moreover, the online success that we see is often carefully curated and meticulously crafted to portray a perfect image. This creates a false sense of reality that can be harmful to both the individuals who are striving for success and those who are consuming the content. It can lead to a never-ending cycle of comparison and self-doubt, where individuals feel like they can never measure up to the idealized versions of themselves that they see online.

It is important to recognize that the illusion of online success is just that - an illusion. It is not a reflection of one's true worth or value as a person. In the following sections of this chapter, we will explore the different facets of online success and the challenges that come along with it. Through this exploration, we hope to shed light on the realities of building an online presence and provide insights on how to navigate this landscape in a healthy and sustainable way.

As social media and online platforms continue to gain popularity, many people are drawn to the idea of starting an online business or becoming an influencer. However, the image of success portrayed on social media can often be an illusion that creates unrealistic expectations.

The pressure to present a perfect image can lead to people feeling like they have to portray a lifestyle that is not authentic. This can lead to feelings of inadequacy and frustration when they do not achieve the level of success they see others achieving online. In turn, this can create a negative cycle where people become more focused on their image rather than their actual work.

Furthermore, the ease of access to social media and online platforms has created a saturated market that makes it difficult for newcomers to break through and gain success. The competition is high, and many people fail to recognize that it takes time, hard work, and dedication to establish a successful online business or brand.

Additionally, the rise of fake followers and fake likes has created a further illusion of success. Many people purchase followers and likes to create the appearance of popularity, but these do not translate into genuine engagement or revenue. This can create a false sense of accomplishment and make it harder for those who are genuinely working hard to achieve success.

Overall, the illusion of online success can have a profound impact on people's attitudes towards starting an online business or influencer brand. It can lead to unrealistic expectations and a focus on image rather than genuine work, making it harder for those who are willing to put in the effort to achieve success. In the following sections, we will explore the various ways in which this illusion of success can be detrimental and the steps that can be taken to overcome it.

The rise of the internet and social media has created an illusion of success that is often unrealistic and unattainable. Many people believe that establishing an online business or influencer brand is an easy way to achieve financial freedom and personal fulfillment. However, the reality is far from this idealized vision. In this chapter, we will explore the challenges and pitfalls of establishing an online business or influencer brand, and provide insight into what it takes to succeed in the digital age.

The Illusion of Success:

The allure of online success is strong, but the reality of achieving it is much more complex. The internet and social media present a distorted view of success, portraying it as effortless and instant. In reality, establishing an online business or influencer brand requires hard work, dedication, and a great deal of strategic planning.

Many people are drawn to the idea of online success because it seems like a shortcut to financial freedom and personal fulfillment. They see others posting glamorous photos on social media, making viral videos, and creating successful businesses, and they want a piece of the pie. However, the truth is that success in the online world is much more complicated than it appears.

Challenges and Pitfalls:

Establishing an online business or influencer brand is not without its challenges and pitfalls. The internet is a crowded and competitive space, and standing out from the crowd requires a great deal of skill, strategy, and creativity.

One of the biggest challenges of building an online business or influencer brand is establishing trust and credibility with potential customers or followers. The internet is rife with scams and fraudulent activity, and many people are wary of trusting businesses or individuals they have never met in person.

Another challenge is the ever-changing landscape of the internet and social media. Trends and algorithms shift constantly, and keeping up with these changes can be overwhelming. In addition, online businesses and influencer brands are subject to the same legal and regulatory requirements as traditional businesses, adding an extra layer of complexity to the mix.

Success in the Digital Age:

Despite the challenges and pitfalls, it is possible to succeed in the online world. The key is to approach online business and influencer branding with a clear understanding of what it takes to succeed.

One of the most important factors for success is authenticity. People are drawn to businesses and individuals who are genuine and transparent in their online presence. Building trust and credibility with potential customers or followers requires honesty, openness, and a willingness to engage with your audience.

Another key factor for success is strategic planning. Establishing an online business or influencer brand requires a well thought-out plan that takes into account your goals, target audience, competition, and resources. This plan should be flexible enough to adapt to changing trends and algorithms, but also focused enough to keep you on track towards your objectives.

The illusion of online success is tempting, but the reality is much more complex. Establishing an online business or influencer brand requires hard work, dedication, and a great deal of strategic planning. However, with the right approach and mindset, it is possible to succeed in the digital age. In the following sections, we will explore the specific challenges and pitfalls of online business and influencer branding, and provide practical advice and insight into what it takes to succeed in this dynamic and ever-changing landscape.

The Reality of Online Business:

As more and more individuals turn to the internet to launch their own businesses and build personal brands, it is important to understand the reality of what it takes to succeed in the digital age. This chapter will delve into the world of online business and influencer brands, exploring the challenges and obstacles that entrepreneurs face and providing insight into how to navigate these hurdles. From the initial stages of launching a business or brand to maintaining success over time, this chapter will offer practical advice and guidance to help readers achieve their goals in the digital landscape.

Starting and growing an online business can be a daunting task, especially in an age where technology is constantly evolving and the competition is fierce. While the internet has opened up new possibilities for entrepreneurship and innovation, it has also created a highly saturated marketplace that can be difficult to navigate.

One of the biggest challenges facing online businesses is competition. With so many new businesses popping up every day, it can be difficult to stand out from the crowd and attract customers. This is especially true in industries that are already heavily saturated, such as fashion, beauty, and technology. In order to succeed in these markets, entrepreneurs must be able to differentiate themselves and offer something truly unique and valuable to their customers.

Another challenge facing online businesses is changing consumer behavior. As the world becomes increasingly digital, consumers are becoming more discerning and demanding in their online interactions. They expect personalized experiences, fast and efficient service, and a seamless shopping experience across multiple platforms. This means that businesses must be able to adapt quickly to changing trends and consumer preferences in order to stay relevant and competitive.

In addition to competition and changing consumer behavior, online businesses also face the challenge of market saturation. With so many businesses vying for the same customers, it can be difficult to break through the noise and make a lasting impression. This is particularly true in industries that are dominated by large, established players. In order to succeed in these markets, entrepreneurs must be able to identify gaps in the market and offer a unique value proposition that sets them apart from the competition.

Despite these challenges, there are many success stories of entrepreneurs who have been able to build thriving online businesses. By focusing on innovation, customer experience, and strategic marketing, these entrepreneurs have been able to carve out their own niche in the digital landscape and achieve success. In the following sections, we will explore some of the strategies and best practices that entrepreneurs can use to overcome the challenges of starting and growing an online business.

In today's digital age, starting an online business seems like a dream come true for many. The allure of being your own boss, setting your own schedule, and earning a passive income is hard to resist. However, the reality of online business is not as simple as it seems.

There are numerous challenges that online business owners face, including competition, market saturation, and changing consumer behavior. These challenges can make it difficult for entrepreneurs to start and grow a successful online business.

One of the biggest challenges for online business owners is competition. With millions of websites and online stores, it can be hard to stand out from the crowd. Many businesses offer similar products and services, making it even more challenging to differentiate yourself and attract customers.

Market saturation is another challenge that online businesses face. Many markets, such as e-commerce and digital marketing, are already saturated with established players. This makes it difficult for new businesses to enter the market and gain traction.

Consumer behavior is constantly changing, which can also pose a challenge for online businesses. It is important to stay up-to-date on the latest trends and preferences of your target audience in order to remain relevant and successful.

To illustrate the challenges of starting and growing an online business, it is helpful to look at examples of businesses that have succeeded and those that have failed. One example of a successful online business is popular e-commerce platform, which started as an online bookstore and has now become one of the world's largest e-commerce platforms. It's success can be attributed to its customer-centric approach and its ability to continuously innovate and expand its offerings.

On the other hand, there are many examples of online businesses that have failed. One such example is the online pet supply store, Pets.com.

Despite a high-profile marketing campaign, the company failed to generate enough revenue to sustain its business and eventually went bankrupt.

Analyzing the factors that contributed to the success or failure of these businesses can provide valuable insights for aspiring online business owners. It is important to identify your unique value proposition, stay up-to-date on industry trends, and constantly innovate in order to stand out from the competition and succeed in the online marketplace.

The internet has made it easier than ever for entrepreneurs to start their own online businesses. However, with more and more people flocking to the digital world, the competition has become fierce. It's not enough to just have a website or social media presence – online business owners need to have a solid strategy and unique value proposition in order to stand out from the crowd. In this chapter, we will explore the reality of online business and the challenges that come with it.

Challenges of Starting and Growing an Online Business: While the internet has opened up a world of opportunities for entrepreneurs, starting an online business is not without its challenges. One of the biggest challenges is competition. With so many businesses vying for attention, it can be difficult to stand out from the crowd. Another challenge is market saturation. Some niches have become so saturated that it's difficult for new businesses to break in. And consumer behavior is constantly changing, making it a challenge to keep up with trends and preferences.

Examples of Online Business Success and Failure: There are countless examples of online businesses that have succeeded and those that have failed. For every success story, there are countless businesses that never made it off the ground. One factor that can contribute to success is having a unique value proposition. Businesses that offer something truly unique and valuable to their target audience are more likely to succeed. On the other hand, businesses that try to copy what others are doing without bringing anything new to the table are less likely to succeed.

Importance of a Solid Business Plan and Value Proposition: Having a solid business plan and a clear understanding of one's target audience is essential for online business success. A business plan should outline the company's goals, strategies, and tactics for achieving those goals. It should also include a detailed analysis of the competition and the market. A unique value proposition is what sets a business apart from its competitors. It should be clear, concise, and compelling, and should highlight what the business offers that others don't.

In conclusion, starting and growing an online business is not for the faint of heart. It takes hard work, dedication, and a solid strategy to succeed in the crowded online marketplace. However, with the right approach and a unique value proposition, it's possible to create a successful online business.

The Truth About Influencer Brands:

In recent years, social media has given rise to a new phenomenon known as the "influencer brand." These are individuals who have built a following on platforms, and who leverage their popularity to promote products and services to their audience. While the idea of making a living by posting pictures or videos online may seem like a dream job, the reality is often far more complicated. In this section, we will explore the truth about influencer brands and the challenges they face in the digital age.

The rise of social media and influencer marketing has created an illusion of success that has lured many individuals into the world of online influence. However, the reality of building a successful influencer brand is much more complex than the glitz and glamour portrayed on social media platforms.

Becoming a successful influencer brand requires a deep understanding of the social media landscape, a creative approach to content creation, and the ability to cultivate and maintain a loyal following. Furthermore, the market for influencer brands is becoming increasingly saturated, making it more difficult than ever to stand out from the crowd.

To succeed as an influencer brand, one must be willing to put in the work and constantly adapt to changing trends and consumer behavior. It is no longer enough to simply post pretty pictures and promote products - audiences today demand authentic, high-quality content that resonates with their values and interests.

In this section, we will explore the challenges and realities of building a successful influencer brand, and provide insight into what it takes to truly succeed in the world of online influence. From the importance of niche marketing to the role of authenticity and transparency, we will delve into the factors that contribute to the success or failure of an influencer brand.

The world of influencer marketing is vast and varied, with countless individuals and brands vying for the attention of an ever-growing audience. While some influencers have achieved incredible success, others have struggled to gain traction, despite putting in a significant amount of time and effort.

When examining the factors that contribute to success in the influencer space, one of the most critical is the ability to build a loyal following. Influencers who can cultivate a community of engaged and dedicated followers are more likely to see long-term success than those who fail to connect with their audience.

Another key challenge for influencers is the need to produce high-quality content that resonates with their followers. With so much content available online, it can be difficult for influencers to stand out from the crowd and make an impact. The most successful influencers are those who can consistently create content that is unique, compelling, and relevant to their audience.

Finally, maintaining authenticity is critical for influencers who want to succeed in a market that can sometimes seem saturated with people trying to sell products or promote their personal brand. Influencers who can remain true to themselves and their values are more likely to build trust and credibility with their followers, which can ultimately lead to greater success.

Despite the challenges, there are countless examples of influencers who have achieved incredible success. From lifestyle bloggers and beauty gurus to fitness experts and food enthusiasts, there is no shortage of people who have leveraged the power of social media to build successful and lucrative influencer brands.

However, for every success story, there are many more individuals who have struggled to gain traction in the competitive world of influencer marketing. Whether due to a lack of engagement with their followers, a failure to produce compelling content, or a perceived lack of authenticity, there are many pitfalls that can derail an influencer's career.

In recent years, the world of influencer branding has exploded, with social media platforms providing fertile ground for creators to build their own brands and connect with audiences around the world. These individuals, known as influencers, have built enormous followings through their creative content, engaging personalities, and powerful messages. From beauty gurus to lifestyle bloggers, there seems to be an influencer for every niche and every interest.

However, despite the glamour and excitement that often surrounds the world of influencer branding, it is also a highly competitive and challenging industry to navigate. In order to succeed, influencers must have a clear understanding of their target audience, a unique voice and style, and the ability to constantly create and produce high-quality content that resonates with their followers.

Some of the most successful influencer brands in the world today have built their success on a combination of talent, hard work, and a willingness to take risks and try new things. Take, for example, fashion and beauty influencer Chiara Ferragni, who has amassed a following of over 23 million on social media and built a successful fashion empire through her popular blog and brand, The Blonde Salad.

Ffor every success story in the world of influencer branding, there are countless examples of individuals who have struggled to make a name for themselves or have fallen prey to the numerous pitfalls that can arise in this industry. From burnout and creative blocks to controversies and scandals, influencers face a wide range of challenges and pressures that can make it difficult to build a sustainable and fulfilling career.

Despite these challenges, the allure of influencer branding remains strong, with many young people inspired by the idea of building their own brand and connecting with audiences on a global scale. Whether you are a seasoned influencer or just starting out in the industry, it is essential to have a clear understanding of the challenges and opportunities that lie ahead, and to approach the world of influencer branding with a realistic and thoughtful mindset.

In today's crowded influencer market, it can be challenging to stand out from the crowd and build a successful brand. However, there are certain strategies that can help aspiring influencers achieve their goals.

One of the key factors in building a successful influencer brand is developing a unique voice and style. This means finding your niche and creating content that is distinctively your own. It's important to differentiate yourself from other influencers in your space by offering something that is new and exciting.

Another important aspect of building a successful influencer brand is building authentic connections with your followers. This means engaging with your audience, responding to comments and messages, and creating content that resonates with your fans. It's important to remember that your followers are real people with real emotions, and that they will respond positively to authenticity and transparency.

Perhaps most importantly, successful influencers are continually innovating and adapting to the ever-changing landscape of social media and digital marketing. This means experimenting with new platforms, trying out new content formats, and staying up-to-date with the latest trends and developments in the industry. It also means being willing to take risks and try new things, even if they don't always work out.

Of course, building a successful influencer brand is not without its challenges and pitfalls. As the market becomes more saturated, it can be increasingly difficult to build a loyal following and maintain relevance. Influencers also face the risk of burnout, as the pressure to constantly produce content and maintain a strong social media presence can be overwhelming.

Moreover, influencers also face the challenge of balancing authenticity with profitability. As brands increasingly turn to influencers for sponsored content and collaborations, there is a risk of losing the trust of followers if they perceive the influencer to be "selling out" or promoting products that don't align with their values.

Despite these challenges, many influencers have been able to build successful and lucrative careers. By developing a unique voice, building authentic connections with followers, and continually innovating, influencers can carve out a niche for themselves in the crowded world of social media and digital marketing.

The Dark Side of Online Success

As the allure of online success continues to grow, it is important to take a closer look at the darker side of this digital landscape. In this chapter, we will explore the hidden challenges and pitfalls that often come with building an online business or influencer brand, and the toll that it can take on one's mental and emotional well-being. From burnout to imposter syndrome to the pressures of maintaining a perfect online persona, we will delve into the psychological and emotional impacts of chasing the illusive dream of online success. Join us as we uncover the truths that are often overlooked in the pursuit of digital fame and fortune.

The digital age has brought about a new era of entrepreneurial opportunities, offering the potential for anyone to build a successful business or brand from the comfort of their own home. However, the pressure to succeed in the online world has resulted in a dark side that is often overlooked. The constant need to stay ahead of the competition, produce high-quality content, and maintain a consistent online presence can take a toll on even the most resilient of individuals.

One of the most significant negative effects of the pressure to succeed online is burnout. Burnout is a state of emotional, physical, and mental exhaustion caused by prolonged stress and overwork. With the always-on culture of the digital world, it can be difficult to switch off and take a break, leading to burnout and its associated symptoms, such as fatigue, cynicism, and reduced productivity.

Another negative effect of the pressure to succeed in the online world is anxiety. The constant need to meet deadlines, produce high-quality content, and maintain a consistent online presence can create a sense of unease and anxiety in even the most confident of individuals. The fear of failure and the pressure to succeed can lead to excessive worry and anxiety, which can have a detrimental effect on mental health and wellbeing.

The pressure to succeed in the online world can also contribute to other mental health issues, such as depression and social isolation. The constant comparison to others, the fear of missing out, and the pressure to maintain a perfect image online can lead to feelings of inadequacy and loneliness.

It is essential to recognize the negative effects of the pressure to succeed in the online world and take steps to mitigate them. This may include setting realistic goals, taking breaks, seeking support from friends and family, and practicing self-care. By recognizing the dark side of online success and taking steps to address it, individuals can achieve their goals while maintaining their mental health and wellbeing.

The pressure to succeed in the online world is not without consequences. Many individuals who have entered this competitive industry have found themselves struggling to keep up with the fast-paced demands and expectations of the digital landscape. From burnout to anxiety and mental health issues, the price of success can sometimes come at a high cost.

One individual who struggled with the pressure to succeed online is Emily, a young entrepreneur who had built a successful e-commerce business from the ground up. After years of hard work and dedication, Emily found herself feeling overwhelmed and exhausted, constantly chasing after the next big thing and striving to maintain her position in the market. Despite her initial success, she began to feel as though she could never truly relax or enjoy her achievements, as there was always more to be done and someone else to compete with.

Emily's story is not uncommon in the online world. The constant pressure to succeed and stay ahead of the competition can take a toll on even the most resilient individuals. The need to constantly produce high-quality content, stay on top of the latest trends, and maintain an engaged and loyal following can leave little room for rest and relaxation.

Other individuals who have struggled with the pressure to succeed online include influencers who have become consumed by the pursuit of followers and likes, entrepreneurs who have sacrificed their personal lives and relationships for the sake of their business, and content creators who have found themselves struggling to keep up with the demands of their audience.

The factors that contribute to these struggles are many and complex. They can include a lack of boundaries and work-life balance, an overemphasis on external validation and success, and a failure to prioritize self-care and mental health. In some cases, individuals may also feel as though they must constantly put on a facade of success and happiness, even if they are struggling behind the scenes.

As the online world continues to grow and evolve, it is essential that we recognize the negative effects of the pressure to succeed and take steps to prioritize our well-being and mental health. Only by addressing these issues can we create a sustainable and fulfilling path to success in the digital age.

The pursuit of online success can be a double-edged sword. On one hand, the ability to reach a global audience and establish oneself as an authority in a particular niche is a thrilling prospect. On the other hand, the pressure to constantly produce high-quality content, build a loyal following, and stay ahead of the competition can be overwhelming and can lead to burnout, anxiety, and other mental health issues.

There have been numerous examples of individuals who have struggled with the pressure to succeed online. In recent years, several high-profile influencers and entrepreneurs have come forward to share their stories of burnout and mental health struggles. This is often due to the demands of running a successful online business or brand, as well as the pressure to constantly produce new and engaging content.

It is clear that the pursuit of online success can have negative consequences on one's mental health. To avoid burnout and other mental health issues, it is important to maintain a healthy work-life balance, set realistic goals, and seek support when needed. This can involve taking breaks from social media and other online activities, practicing self-care, and seeking out resources such as therapy or support groups.

In conclusion, while the online world offers countless opportunities for success, it is important to remember that there are also challenges and risks involved. By prioritizing our mental health and taking steps to avoid burnout, we can pursue our online goals in a healthy and sustainable way.

Navigating the Illusion of Online Success

In today's digital age, the idea of success has taken on a whole new meaning, with online influencers and businesses seemingly able to achieve overnight success and fame. However, the reality is often far more complex and challenging than the illusion of success that is presented online. In this section, we will explore the tools and strategies that can help individuals navigate the often confusing and overwhelming world of online success, while avoiding the pitfalls and challenges that come with it. From developing a clear and realistic plan, to maintaining a focus on authenticity and connection with one's audience, we will examine the key factors that contribute to a successful and sustainable online presence.

Navigating the Illusion of Online Success can be a challenging task for anyone looking to establish an online business or influencer brand. While the digital age has opened up new opportunities for entrepreneurs and content creators, it has also created a crowded and competitive marketplace where success can be elusive. In this section, we will provide practical advice and strategies for navigating this landscape and avoiding the pitfalls of the illusion of online success.

One of the most important strategies for navigating the online world is to have a clear understanding of one's goals and objectives. This involves defining what success means to you and setting realistic expectations for achieving it. It is also important to have a solid business plan and a unique value proposition that sets you apart from the competition. This will help you to establish a clear brand identity and build a loyal following.

Another key strategy for success in the online world is to maintain authenticity and transparency in all your interactions with followers and customers. This means being honest about your strengths and weaknesses, and avoiding the temptation to present a perfect image of yourself or your brand. It also means being open and transparent about how you operate your business, and being willing to listen to feedback and criticism from your audience.

Networking and collaboration are also important strategies for navigating the online world. Building relationships with other entrepreneurs, influencers, and industry experts can help you to gain valuable insights into your market, and may lead to opportunities for collaboration and partnership. It is also important to be willing to learn and adapt as the online landscape evolves, and to be open to new ideas and approaches.

Finally, it is important to maintain a healthy work-life balance and to take care of your mental and physical well-being. The pressure to succeed in the online world can be overwhelming at times, and it is important to prioritize self-care and to seek support when needed. This may involve setting boundaries around work and social media use, taking breaks and vacations, and seeking professional help when necessary.

Navigating the Illusion of Online Success requires a combination of practical skills, emotional resilience, and a clear sense of purpose. By developing a solid business plan, maintaining authenticity and transparency, networking and collaborating with others, and prioritizing self-care and well-being, you can increase your chances of success in the digital age.

As the online landscape continues to evolve and shift, it can be difficult to navigate the illusion of online success. For those looking to establish an online business or become a successful influencer brand, it is essential to approach the process with a realistic mindset and a solid plan.

One key element of navigating the illusion of online success is being honest with oneself about goals and expectations. While it can be tempting to set unrealistic expectations and goals based on the successes of others, it is important to remember that each individual's journey is unique. It is crucial to take the time to reflect on what success means to you personally, and to set achievable goals that align with your values and vision.

Another important strategy is seeking advice and support from trusted sources. This can include mentorship from experienced entrepreneurs or influencers, as well as seeking out online communities and resources that can offer guidance and support. It is important to approach this process with an open mind and a willingness to learn and grow.

Continuously learning and adapting to changing trends and markets is also essential for navigating the illusion of online success. This means staying up to date on the latest developments in your industry, as well as keeping an eye on emerging technologies and trends that may impact your business or brand. It is important to be proactive in exploring new opportunities and experimenting with different approaches in order to stay relevant and competitive.

Ultimately, the key to navigating the illusion of online success is approaching the process with a realistic and flexible mindset, seeking out support and guidance, and continuously learning and adapting. By embracing these strategies, individuals can build a solid foundation for their online businesses or influencer brands, and avoid the pitfalls of the illusion of online success.

In conclusion, the online world presents incredible opportunities for those who are willing to put in the work to establish a successful business or influencer brand. However, it is important to remember that the illusion of online success can be deceiving and often unrealistic. It is crucial to approach online entrepreneurship with a realistic understanding of the challenges and pitfalls that come with it.

By exploring the challenges of starting and growing an online business or influencer brand, as well as the negative effects of the pressure to succeed online, this chapter has provided valuable insight into what it takes to succeed in the digital age. By understanding the reality of online business and the truth about influencer brands, readers can better navigate the online landscape and avoid the pitfalls of the illusion of online success.

To succeed in the online world, it is important to have a solid business plan, a unique value proposition, and a clear understanding of one's target audience. It is equally important to maintain a healthy work-life balance, set realistic goals, seek advice and support, and continuously learn and adapt to changing trends and markets.

By following these strategies and staying grounded in reality, readers can increase their chances of success in the online world while avoiding the negative effects of the pressure to succeed. The online landscape can be both exciting and challenging, but with the right mindset and approach, anyone can achieve their goals and thrive in the digital age.

The Business of Influencing

In today's world, the rise of social media and the internet has given birth to a new form of marketing - influencer marketing. Influencers, who have a large and dedicated following on social media platforms, have become an essential part of many companies' marketing strategies. Influencer marketing has become a billion-dollar industry, with businesses investing significant amounts of money in influencer collaborations to reach their target audience and increase brand awareness.

However, the influencer industry is not all glitz and glamour, as it may seem on the surface. Behind the filters and perfectly curated posts, there is a business side to influencing that can be challenging to navigate. In this chapter, we will delve into the business of influencing, exploring the opportunities and challenges of being an influencer and working with them. We will provide insights into the different aspects of the industry, including negotiating brand deals, building a personal brand, and managing content creation.

While influencer marketing can seem like an easy way to make a quick buck, it requires a lot of hard work, dedication, and creativity to succeed. Aspiring influencers must be prepared to put in long hours, take risks, and continually adapt to changing trends and algorithms. Brands, on the other hand, must be discerning when selecting influencers to work with and be willing to invest in long-term partnerships that align with their brand values.

The purpose of this chapter is to provide a comprehensive overview of the business of influencing, highlighting the challenges and opportunities that come with being an influencer and partnering with them. We hope to provide valuable insights and practical advice for anyone interested in pursuing a career in influencing or working with influencers as part of their marketing strategy. So let's dive into the world of influencing and explore what it takes to succeed in this dynamic and rapidly evolving industry.

The Evolution of Influencer Marketing:

The rise of influencer marketing has been nothing short of meteoric, transforming the way that companies advertise and consumers shop. It's hard to imagine a world without influencers promoting products and experiences, but the truth is that this type of marketing is relatively new. In this section, we will explore the evolution of influencer marketing, from its early beginnings to the massive industry it is today.

The roots of influencer marketing can be traced back to the early days of social media. Before the widespread use of platforms, blogs were the primary way that influencers shared their thoughts and ideas with their audiences. Some of the earliest influencers were fashion bloggers like BryanBoy and Susie Lau, who gained significant followings through their unique sense of style and engaging content.

As social media platforms began to emerge and gain popularity, influencers quickly adapted and began using them to expand their reach. The rise of some social media platform in particular was a game-changer for influencer marketing, as the platform's visual nature made it ideal for sharing lifestyle content and showcasing products. The rise of video platforms also played a significant role, as video content became an increasingly popular way for influencers to engage with their audiences.

Over the years, the influencer marketing industry has continued to grow and evolve. In 2010, the Federal Trade Commission (FTC) in the United States released guidelines for endorsements and testimonials in advertising, which included rules for sponsored content on social media. This was a significant step towards regulating the industry and ensuring that consumers were aware of when influencers were being paid to promote products.

As influencer marketing became more mainstream, brands began to take notice and invest heavily in this type of advertising. According to a 2019 report by Business Insider Intelligence, the influencer marketing industry was projected to be worth $8 billion by 2020. This growth has been driven by a number of factors, including the increasing importance of social media in consumers' lives, the decline of traditional advertising methods, and the ability of influencers to connect with niche audiences.

In this section, we will delve deeper into the evolution of influencer marketing and the factors that have contributed to its growth and success. We will examine the changing landscape of social media and how this has impacted the influencer industry, as well as the role that regulation and ethics play in the world of influencer marketing. We will also look at the future of influencer marketing and what we can expect in the years to come.

Influencer marketing has evolved dramatically over the years, and with it, so have the types of influencers that have emerged in the industry. From macro-influencers with millions of followers to micro-influencers with a smaller but more engaged audience, there is no shortage of individuals looking to make their mark in the digital space. In this section, we will explore the different types of influencers that exist and their unique roles in the industry.

1. Celebrities:
   Celebrities have long been used as endorsers for brands, and the same holds true in the digital age. Celebrities have a large following and significant influence, making them valuable

partners for brands looking to reach a broader audience. However, the cost of working with a celebrity can be prohibitively high, and their involvement may not always feel authentic to their followers.

2. Macro-influencers:

   Macro-influencers are individuals with a large following, typically ranging from 100,000 to millions of followers. They are often considered to be the most recognizable type of influencer and can be found across various social media platforms. Macro-influencers are often sought after by brands for their reach and ability to generate buzz around a product or service.

3. Micro-influencers:

   Micro-influencers are individuals with a smaller but highly engaged following, typically ranging from 1,000 to 100,000 followers. They often specialize in a particular niche or topic and are known for their authenticity and ability to connect with their audience on a more personal level. While their reach may be smaller than that of macro-influencers, their engagement rates are often higher, making them an attractive option for brands looking to target a specific audience.

4. Nano-influencers:

   Nano-influencers are individuals with a very small following, typically ranging from 500 to 5,000 followers. They are often considered to be the most niche type of influencer, with their content often catering to a very specific audience. While their reach may be limited, their engagement rates are typically high, and they are known for their ability to drive sales through word-of-mouth marketing.

5. Brand ambassadors:

   Brand ambassadors are influencers who have a long-term relationship with a brand, typically receiving a steady stream of sponsored content and products in exchange for their support. They are often viewed as extensions of the brand and work to promote its products or services to their followers.

6. Employee influencers:

Employee influencers are individuals who work for a particular brand but also have a significant following on social media. They often promote the brand's products or services on their personal channels, acting as a bridge between the brand and their followers.

7. Advocates:
   Advocates are individuals who are passionate about a particular brand or product and promote it organically without any compensation. They are often considered to be the most authentic type of influencer and can be valuable allies in generating positive word-of-mouth marketing.

Each type of influencer has its unique strengths and weaknesses, and brands must carefully consider their goals and target audience when choosing whom to partner with. Macro-influencers may be ideal for generating buzz and reaching a broad audience, while micro-influencers may be better suited for targeting a specific niche. Nano-influencers, on the other hand, may be valuable in generating authentic word-of-mouth marketing. By understanding the different types of influencers available, brands can make informed decisions about whom to partner with and how best to leverage their influence.

In recent years, the influencer marketing industry has experienced explosive growth, with businesses spending billions of dollars on influencer collaborations and sponsorships. According to a report by Influencer Marketing Hub, the industry is set to reach $13.8 billion in value by 2021, up from $9.7 billion in 2020.

The impact of influencer marketing on businesses is significant. Influencers are able to provide a level of trust and authenticity that traditional advertising cannot match. Consumers are increasingly wary of traditional advertising methods, such as banner ads and pop-ups, and are instead seeking out more personalized and genuine content. By partnering with influencers who have a strong following and a loyal audience, businesses are able to tap into this desire for authenticity and connect with potential customers on a deeper level.

The benefits of influencer marketing are not limited to businesses alone, however. Influencers themselves have been able to turn their personal brand into a lucrative business, with some of the biggest names in the industry earning millions of dollars through sponsored content and collaborations.

In addition, consumers are also able to benefit from the influencer industry. By following their favorite influencers, consumers are able to discover new products and services that they may not have otherwise known about. Influencers are often seen as trusted sources of information and recommendations, making their endorsements highly sought after by both businesses and consumers.

However, with the growth of the industry comes new challenges and concerns. As more and more influencers enter the market, competition has become fierce, and many are resorting to unethical tactics such as buying followers or engagement. This has led to a lack of transparency and trust in the industry, with consumers and businesses alike questioning the authenticity of influencer endorsements.

Furthermore, as the industry continues to grow, there is a risk of oversaturation. With so many influencers vying for attention, it can be difficult for businesses to stand out and for consumers to navigate the overwhelming amount of content available.

As the influencer industry continues to evolve, it is important for businesses, influencers, and consumers to stay informed and aware of the challenges and opportunities that come with it. While there are certainly risks and concerns, the potential for authentic and effective marketing collaborations is undeniable. By working together and approaching the industry with transparency and ethics, the influencer marketing industry can continue to grow and thrive in a sustainable and beneficial way for all involved.

Building Your Brand as an Influencer

As social media platforms continue to grow and evolve, the world of influencer marketing has become an increasingly popular way for individuals to monetize their online presence. Becoming a successful influencer requires much more than just having a large following, however. It requires dedication, creativity, and a strategic approach to building a personal brand that resonates with your audience. In this section, we will explore the key steps involved in building your brand as an influencer, including identifying your niche, developing your content strategy, and building your personal brand identity.

As the influencer industry continues to grow and evolve, building a strong personal brand has become a crucial aspect of success in the industry. Personal branding is the process of creating and maintaining an identity that reflects one's values, beliefs, and unique qualities. In the context of influencer marketing, it involves crafting a public persona that resonates with a target audience and helps to build a loyal following.

One of the key reasons why building a personal brand is so important for influencers is that it helps to differentiate them from their competitors. With so many influencers vying for attention in the crowded social media space, having a distinct brand identity can help to make an influencer stand out and attract a dedicated following.

Another important benefit of building a personal brand is that it can help to establish an influencer as a thought leader in their niche or industry. By consistently sharing valuable content and insights, an influencer can position themselves as an expert and gain the trust and respect of their audience.

In order to build a successful personal brand, influencers need to have a clear understanding of their target audience and what they are looking for. This involves conducting market research, identifying trends and gaps in the market, and creating content that resonates with their audience.

It's also important for influencers to be authentic and transparent in their branding efforts. This means being honest about one's values and beliefs, and avoiding the temptation to present a false or idealized image of oneself. Influencers who are genuine and authentic are more likely to build a loyal and engaged following.

Certainly. Building a personal brand as an influencer is essential to standing out in a crowded market and gaining a loyal following. It involves creating a unique identity that is authentic and relatable to the target audience.

To start building a personal brand, it's important to identify your niche and target audience. This involves determining what topics you are knowledgeable and passionate about and what audience would be interested in those topics. It's important to narrow down the focus and not try to appeal to everyone.

Next, it's important to create a consistent visual identity across all platforms. This includes having a cohesive color scheme, font, and visual elements that align with your brand values and target audience. It's also important to have a clear and concise bio that showcases your expertise and personality.

Another crucial aspect of building a personal brand is creating high-quality content that resonates with your target audience. This involves creating content that is engaging, informative, and visually appealing. It's important to stay on top of current trends and adapt your content strategy accordingly.

Finally, building a personal brand also involves engaging with your audience and building relationships with them. This can involve responding to comments, direct messages, and emails, as well as collaborating with other influencers and brands in your niche. Building a strong relationship with your audience can lead to increased brand loyalty and ultimately, greater success as an influencer.

Meet Sarah, a 25-year-old aspiring influencer. Sarah had always been interested in beauty and fashion and loved sharing her style with friends and family. She started posting her outfits and makeup looks on social media, and soon found that she had a small following of people who were interested in her content.

Excited by the prospect of turning her hobby into a career, Sarah began to research how to become a successful influencer. She spent hours each day scrolling through her favorite influencer's pages, studying their content, and trying to figure out what made them successful.

Sarah quickly realized that building a personal brand was key to becoming a successful influencer. She started to curate her content more carefully, making sure that each post fit into her overall brand aesthetic. She also started to engage more with her followers, responding to comments and direct messages and building a loyal community.

Over time, Sarah's following grew, and she began to receive invitations to collaborate with brands. She was thrilled to receive her first paid partnership offer, and worked hard to create content that she knew her audience would love.

Despite the success she had achieved, Sarah often felt pressure to constantly produce new and engaging content. She found that she was spending more and more time on social media, and was struggling to balance her influencer career with her personal life.

Sarah's story is just one example of the challenges and rewards of building a personal brand as an influencer. Like any business venture, it requires hard work, dedication, and a willingness to constantly adapt to changing trends and markets. However, for those who are able to succeed, the rewards can be great.

Influencers have become a vital part of the marketing industry, and their strategies for building their brands and growing their following have become increasingly important. Here are some of the key strategies used by successful influencers:

1. Consistent and high-quality content: Consistency is key in the world of influencers. They need to create and publish high-quality content that resonates with their target audience. This means understanding their audience's interests, preferences, and behaviors and creating content that speaks to them.

2. Authenticity and transparency: Influencers need to be authentic and transparent in their content and interactions with their followers. This means being honest about sponsored posts and disclosing any partnerships or collaborations. Authenticity and transparency help build trust and credibility with their followers, which is essential for long-term success.

3. Engaging with their audience: Successful influencers actively engage with their audience by responding to comments and messages, hosting live streams and Q&A sessions, and encouraging feedback and participation. This creates a sense of community and strengthens the bond between the influencer and their followers.

4. Leveraging multiple social media platforms: Successful influencers often have a presence on multiple social media platforms and use them strategically to reach a wider audience. For example, they may use reels for visual content, short messaging for real-time updates and conversations, and video platforms for longer-form videos.

5. Collaborating with other influencers and brands: Collaborations with other influencers and brands can help an influencer reach a new audience and build credibility. This can take the form of sponsored content, joint giveaways, or even co-creating content.

6. Staying on top of trends and new platforms: Successful influencers need to stay up-to-date with the latest trends and platforms in the industry. This means regularly experimenting with new features and platforms, testing out new types of content, and keeping an eye on emerging trends.

7. Providing value to their audience: Ultimately, influencers need to provide value to their audience in order to maintain their following. This could mean offering helpful tips, providing

entertainment, or sharing personal stories and insights. By providing value, influencers can build a loyal and engaged audience.

It's important to note that these strategies are not a one-size-fits-all solution. Influencers need to tailor their strategies to their unique brand and audience. What works for one influencer may not work for another, and it's important to experiment and find what works best for their brand and audience.

In conclusion, the strategies used by successful influencers to build their brands and grow their following are multifaceted and require a lot of time, effort, and experimentation. However, by consistently creating high-quality content, being authentic and transparent, engaging with their audience, leveraging multiple social media platforms, collaborating with other influencers and brands, staying on top of trends, and providing value to their audience, influencers can build a strong and engaged following and achieve long-term success in the industry.

Some practical advice:

Becoming a successful influencer takes time, effort, and dedication. Here are some practical tips to help you develop your own unique brand:

1. Define your niche: The first step to building your personal brand as an influencer is to define your niche. This is the area of expertise or interest that you will focus on and become known for. Consider your passions, skills, and experience to determine what niche you can bring the most value to.

2. Identify your target audience: Knowing who your audience is will help you tailor your content and marketing strategies to their interests and preferences. Conduct research to understand the demographics, interests, and behavior of your target audience.

3. Develop a unique voice and style: Your personality and voice are what will set you apart from other influencers in your niche. Experiment with different styles of content to find what works best for you and your audience.

4. Produce high-quality content: The quality of your content is critical to building a strong following and gaining credibility as an influencer. Invest in high-quality equipment, such as a camera or microphone, and edit your content carefully to ensure it is visually appealing and engaging.

5. Be authentic and transparent: Authenticity is key to building trust with your audience. Be transparent about your experiences, opinions, and any sponsorships or partnerships you have. This will help you build a loyal following who values your authenticity.

6. Engage with your audience: Responding to comments and messages, hosting live Q&A sessions, and creating polls and surveys are effective ways to engage with your audience and build a strong community.

7. Collaborate with other influencers and brands: Collaborating with other influencers and brands can help you expand your reach and gain new followers. Look for opportunities to collaborate with influencers who have a similar target audience or complementary niche.

8. Continuously learn and adapt: The world of social media and influencer marketing is constantly evolving. Stay up to date on industry trends, changes in algorithms, and new platforms to ensure that you are always growing and improving.

Building a personal brand as an influencer takes time and effort, but by following these tips, you can establish yourself as a credible and influential voice in your niche.

Navigating the Business of Influencing

The world of influencing has rapidly evolved over the past few years, with more and more individuals seeking to establish themselves as influencers in their respective niches. The opportunities and potential rewards in this industry are immense, but so too are the challenges and pitfalls. Navigating the business of influencing requires a deep understanding of the industry, a strong work ethic, and a willingness to continuously adapt and grow. In this section, we will explore the strategies and tactics used by successful influencers to navigate this ever-changing landscape and build long-term, sustainable careers. We will also examine the common challenges and pitfalls that influencers face, and provide practical advice for overcoming these obstacles and achieving success in the industry.

Influencer marketing may seem glamorous from the outside, but it is not without its challenges and pitfalls. One of the primary challenges is the need to constantly create and share engaging content that resonates with followers. This requires a great deal of time, effort, and creativity. Influencers must also stay up-to-date with trends and adapt their content to changing market demands in order to maintain relevance and grow their following.

Another challenge is the competitive nature of the industry. With so many influencers vying for attention, it can be difficult to stand out and attract brand partnerships. This can lead to a sense of pressure to constantly produce content and grow one's following, which can be mentally and emotionally exhausting.

Additionally, influencers often face criticism and scrutiny from both their followers and the general public. They may be accused of being inauthentic or "selling out" if they partner with too many brands, or may face backlash for promoting products or services that are not well-received by their audience.

Furthermore, influencers must navigate the business side of the industry, which includes negotiating partnerships and contracts, managing finances, and protecting their personal brand and reputation. This requires a certain level of business acumen and can be overwhelming for those who are not prepared.

It is also worth noting that working as an influencer can be isolating, as it often involves working alone and communicating primarily through digital platforms. This can be a challenge for those who thrive on social interaction and collaboration.

In order to succeed as an influencer, it is important to be aware of these challenges and develop strategies for overcoming them. This may include setting boundaries around work hours and content creation, seeking support and advice from other influencers and industry professionals, and prioritizing self-care to maintain mental and emotional well-being.

As influencer marketing has become a multi-billion dollar industry, sponsored content has become a common part of the influencer business model. However, this can create a dilemma for influencers, as they must balance the need to make a living with the desire to maintain their authenticity and credibility with their followers.

The Federal Trade Commission (FTC) requires that influencers disclose any sponsored content, but this has not stopped some influencers from trying to hide or downplay their sponsorships. This lack of transparency can erode trust with followers and ultimately damage an influencer's brand.

Successful influencers understand the importance of maintaining authenticity and transparency in sponsored content. They carefully select brands and products that align with their personal values and interests, and they disclose their partnerships with complete transparency.

In addition to maintaining authenticity in sponsored content, influencers must also navigate the business side of their work. This includes negotiating contracts, managing finances, and building relationships with brands and agencies.

As the industry becomes more competitive and saturated, influencers must also adapt to changing trends and market demands. They must continually innovate and find new ways to stand out in a crowded marketplace.

To navigate these challenges, aspiring influencers should focus on building a strong personal brand and creating high-quality content that resonates with their target audience. They should also prioritize transparency and authenticity in all their partnerships and collaborations, and continually work to build and maintain strong relationships with brands and agencies.

In addition, influencers should take a strategic approach to the business side of their work, seeking out opportunities to grow and diversify their revenue streams, while also carefully managing their finances and negotiating fair contracts.

Overall, the influencer industry presents many challenges and pitfalls, but with a strategic approach and a commitment to authenticity and transparency, it is possible to succeed and build a successful career as an influencer.

Influencer marketing has grown into a lucrative industry, and as such, influencers need to be savvy negotiators when it comes to working with brands. Here are some practical tips for negotiating with brands, setting rates, and building long-term partnerships.

1. Determine your worth: Before negotiating with brands, you need to know your worth as an influencer. This includes understanding your audience demographics, engagement rate, and the value you can offer to a brand. There are several online tools available that can help you determine your worth, such as Influencer Marketing Hub and Social Bluebook.
2. Be flexible: While it's important to have a set rate card, it's also important to be flexible when negotiating with brands. Every brand has different goals and budgets, so you need to be able to adapt to their needs. You may need to negotiate on price, but be sure to keep your worth in mind.

3. Build relationships: Building long-term partnerships with brands is key to a successful influencer career. It's important to cultivate relationships with brands you genuinely love and use their products. These types of partnerships can lead to ongoing collaborations and increased rates.

4. Have a contract: Always have a contract in place when working with brands. This ensures that both parties are clear on the deliverables, timelines, and payment terms. Contracts also protect you from any misunderstandings or miscommunications.

5. Deliver quality content: One of the most important aspects of working with brands is delivering high-quality content that aligns with their goals and values. Take the time to understand the brand's message and create content that resonates with your audience.

6. Stay organized: As an influencer, you will likely be working with multiple brands at once. It's important to stay organized and keep track of deliverables, timelines, and payment schedules. This will help ensure that you meet all of your obligations and maintain positive relationships with brands.

7. Don't compromise your values: Finally, it's important to maintain your authenticity and not compromise your values for a brand partnership. Your audience trusts you and expects you to be genuine, so it's important to only work with brands that align with your personal brand and values.

In conclusion, negotiating with brands and building long-term partnerships is a crucial aspect of being a successful influencer. By knowing your worth, being flexible, building relationships, having a contract, delivering quality content, staying organized, and not compromising your values, you can navigate the business of influencing with confidence and success.

Legal and Ethical Considerations

In recent years, the influencer industry has exploded in popularity, with brands and consumers alike embracing the power of social media and the personalities behind it. With the rise of influencer marketing, however, comes a new set of legal and ethical considerations that must be considered.

As influencers become more mainstream and their impact on consumer behavior grows, it's important for both influencers and brands to understand the legal and ethical guidelines that govern their relationships. This includes regulations around sponsored content, the use of endorsements and testimonials, and the disclosure of financial relationships between influencers and brands.

The goal of this section is to provide a comprehensive overview of the legal and ethical considerations that must be considered when working as an influencer, and to offer practical advice on how to navigate these complex issues.

As the influencer industry continues to evolve and mature, it's becoming increasingly important for influencers to understand the legal and ethical landscape in which they operate. By taking a proactive approach and staying informed on the latest developments and regulations, influencers can build strong and sustainable careers while maintaining the trust and loyalty of their followers.

In recent years, there has been growing concern about the legal and ethical implications of influencer marketing. As the industry continues to grow and evolve, it is important for both influencers and brands to understand the rules and regulations that apply to them.

One of the most important legal considerations for influencers is the requirement to disclose sponsored content. In many countries, including the United States and United Kingdom, it is mandatory for influencers to disclose when they have received compensation for promoting a product or service. This can be done through clear and conspicuous language such as #ad or #sponsored.

Failure to disclose sponsored content can result in serious consequences, including fines and damage to one's reputation. In addition to legal requirements, there are also ethical considerations at play. Consumers rely on influencers to provide honest and trustworthy recommendations, and failing to disclose sponsored content can undermine that trust.

Another legal consideration for influencers is the use of copyrighted material. It is important for influencers to obtain permission from the copyright holder before using any images, music, or other creative works in their content. Failure to do so can result in legal action and fines.

In addition to legal considerations, there are also ethical considerations to take into account. Influencers have a responsibility to ensure that their content is truthful and not misleading. This includes disclosing any material connections with brands, as well as being transparent about the results that can be expected from using a product or service.

Furthermore, influencers have a responsibility to ensure that their content is not harmful or offensive to any individual or group. This includes avoiding the use of discriminatory language or imagery, as well as refraining from promoting products or services that may be harmful to one's health or well-being.

As the influencer marketing industry continues to evolve, it is important for both influencers and brands to stay up-to-date on the latest legal and ethical considerations. This may involve working with legal professionals or industry experts to ensure that all content is compliant with relevant laws and regulations.

In summary, the legal and ethical considerations of influencer marketing are an important aspect of the industry that cannot be overlooked. It is essential for influencers and brands alike to understand the rules and regulations that apply to them, and to take steps to ensure that their content is truthful, transparent, and responsible.

Governments and social media platforms have taken steps to regulate and provide guidelines for influencer marketing. These regulations and guidelines are aimed at ensuring transparency and preventing deceptive advertising practices that may mislead consumers.

In the United States, the Federal Trade Commission (FTC) has released guidelines for influencer marketing, requiring influencers to disclose any paid partnerships or sponsorships. This includes clear and conspicuous disclosures in the post or video itself, as well as in the profile bio or link. The FTC has also made it clear that the responsibility of disclosure falls on both the influencer and the brand, and failure to comply may result in legal action.

Similarly, in the European Union, the General Data Protection Regulation (GDPR) requires influencers to obtain explicit consent from their followers before collecting and using their personal data for marketing purposes. In addition, the Advertising Standards Authority (ASA) in the UK has released guidelines for influencer marketing, stating that all sponsored content must be clearly labeled as such and must not be misleading to consumers.

Social media platforms have also implemented their own guidelines and features to ensure transparency in influencer marketing. Some platforms has introduced a "paid partnership" feature, which allows influencers to tag the brand they are working with and provides a clear disclosure to the audience. Some other platforms has a similar feature called "paid promotion," which requires influencers to disclose any paid partnerships in the video description.

Despite these regulations and guidelines, there have been instances of influencers and brands failing to disclose sponsored content, leading to criticism and legal action. In 2019, the FTC settled with creator Trevor "TmarTn" Martin and website owner Thomas "Syndicate" Cassell for not disclosing their ownership of a gambling site they were promoting on their channels. This case served as a warning to influencers and brands that failure to disclose sponsored content may have legal consequences.

In addition to legal regulations, there are also ethical considerations in influencer marketing. Influencers have a responsibility to be honest and transparent with their audience, and not to promote products or services that they do not truly believe in or that may be harmful to their followers. Brands also have a responsibility to ensure that their products or services are safe and ethical, and not to pressure influencers into promoting their products in a misleading way.

Overall, it is important for influencers and brands to stay informed of the regulations and guidelines set forth by government agencies and social media platforms, and to prioritize transparency and honesty in their marketing practices. By doing so, they can build trust with their audience and maintain the integrity of the influencer marketing industry.

In today's fast-paced digital world, influencer marketing has become an essential component of brand awareness and product promotion. With the rise of social media platforms, influencers have become key players in the marketing game, with their ability to engage and sway their followers to take action.

However, with great power comes great responsibility. As influencers navigate the business of influencing, it is important for them to keep in mind the legal and ethical considerations of their work. Failure to do so can result in damaging consequences, not only for the influencer but for the brands they work with and the consumers they interact with.

In this section, we will analyze the legal and ethical considerations of influencer marketing and provide practical advice for influencers on how to maintain legal and ethical standards.

Legal Considerations:

The Federal Trade Commission (FTC) has established guidelines for influencer marketing to ensure that consumers are not deceived or misled by sponsored content. These guidelines require influencers to clearly disclose their relationship with brands when promoting products or services on social media platforms. Failure to do so can result in legal action by the FTC.

In addition, influencers must adhere to copyright laws when creating content. This means obtaining permission or licensing for the use of copyrighted material, such as music or images, in their content.

Ethical Considerations:

In addition to legal considerations, influencers must also consider the ethical implications of their work. Influencers hold a significant amount of influence over their followers and have the power to shape their opinions and behaviors. As such, they must use their platform responsibly and with integrity.

One ethical consideration is the use of photoshop or filters to alter their appearance. This can create unrealistic beauty standards and perpetuate a harmful beauty culture. It is important for influencers to promote body positivity and self-love by embracing their natural beauty and using their platform to promote diversity and inclusivity.

Another ethical consideration is the promotion of products that may be harmful to their followers, such as weight loss supplements or skincare products with questionable ingredients. Influencers must thoroughly research the products they promote and ensure they align with their personal values and beliefs.

Practical Advice:

To maintain legal and ethical standards, influencers should take the following practical steps:

1. Clearly disclose sponsored content: Influencers should clearly disclose their relationship with brands when promoting products or services on social media platforms. This can be done using hashtags such as #ad or #sponsored.

2. Research products and brands: Influencers should thoroughly research the products and brands they promote and ensure they align with their personal values and beliefs.
3. Use photoshopped or filtered images sparingly: Influencers should use their platform to promote body positivity and self-love by embracing their natural beauty and using their platform to promote diversity and inclusivity.
4. Stay up to date with regulations and guidelines: Influencers should stay informed about the latest regulations and guidelines set forth by government agencies and social media platforms to ensure compliance with legal standards.

Influencers must carefully navigate the legal and ethical considerations of their work to maintain their credibility and protect their followers. By taking practical steps to maintain legal and ethical standards, influencers can establish themselves as trusted and respected figures in the industry.

The Future of Influencer Marketing

Influencer marketing has come a long way since its inception. The rise of social media has given birth to a whole new industry, with influencers playing a key role in shaping consumer behavior and driving sales for brands. However, with the ever-changing landscape of social media and the increasing scrutiny on influencer marketing practices, it's important to look towards the future and analyze the potential for growth and change within the industry.

In this section, we will explore the latest trends and predictions for the future of influencer marketing. We will look at the potential impact of emerging technologies, changing consumer behavior, and evolving regulations on the industry. Additionally, we will discuss the opportunities and challenges that lie ahead for influencers and brands alike.

As influencer marketing continues to evolve, it's crucial for both influencers and brands to stay informed and adapt to new trends and practices. In this section, we will provide insights and recommendations on how to stay ahead of the curve and thrive in the ever-changing landscape of influencer marketing.

As the world continues to move towards a more digital age, influencer marketing is poised to play an increasingly significant role in the business world. The industry has already experienced rapid growth and evolution in recent years, with brands and businesses recognizing the power of social media influencers to reach new audiences and drive sales.

However, as with any industry, there are challenges and potential pitfalls that must be addressed in order to ensure continued growth and success. In this section, we will explore the future of influencer marketing, examining the trends and developments that are likely to shape the industry in the years to come.

One major trend that is likely to continue is the rise of micro-influencers. These are influencers with smaller followings, typically in the range of 10,000 to 100,000 followers. While they may not have the massive reach of celebrity influencers, they often have a more engaged and dedicated following, with higher rates of interaction and conversion.

As businesses increasingly look for more targeted and effective marketing strategies, micro-influencers are likely to become even more important. They offer a more affordable and accessible option for businesses of all sizes, and can help to build brand awareness and loyalty among specific audiences.

Another trend to watch is the increasing use of video content, particularly on video platforms. Video has become an incredibly popular and effective way to engage with audiences, and influencers who are able to create high-quality, engaging video content are likely to be in high demand.

However, as video content becomes more prevalent, influencers will also need to be mindful of ethical and legal considerations, particularly around the use of copyrighted materials and the disclosure of sponsored content.

In addition to these trends, there are also likely to be significant developments in the tools and platforms used for influencer marketing. Social media platforms are constantly evolving, with new features and capabilities being added all the time.

As these platforms become more sophisticated and offer more targeted advertising options, businesses and influencers alike will need to stay up to date and adapt their strategies accordingly. This may require a greater emphasis on data analysis and measurement, as well as a willingness to experiment with new approaches and techniques.

Finally, it is worth considering the potential impact of emerging technologies like virtual and augmented reality on influencer marketing. These technologies offer exciting new opportunities for immersive and engaging experiences, but they also raise important questions around privacy, consent, and ethical considerations.

Overall, the future of influencer marketing is likely to be both exciting and challenging. As the industry continues to evolve and mature, it will be important for businesses and influencers alike to stay on top of emerging trends, maintain high ethical and legal standards, and continue to deliver engaging and effective content to their audiences.

In recent years, the influencer marketing industry has experienced explosive growth and has become a multi-billion-dollar industry. As the industry continues to evolve, new trends and technologies are emerging that are shaping the future of influencer marketing.

One major trend in the industry is the shift towards micro-influencers. Micro-influencers are individuals who have a smaller but highly engaged following, typically between 1,000 and 100,000 followers. These influencers are often more niche-focused and are seen as more authentic and relatable to their followers. Brands are increasingly turning to micro-influencers to reach specific audiences and achieve higher engagement rates.

Another emerging trend is the rise of video content. Video platforms are driving the demand for short-form video content, and influencers are adapting to this trend by creating more video-based content. Video content allows influencers to showcase products in a more engaging and creative way, and is expected to become even more important in the future of influencer marketing.

In addition to these trends, new technologies are also playing a role in shaping the future of the industry. Augmented reality (AR) and virtual reality (VR) technologies are allowing influencers to create more immersive and interactive content for their followers. These technologies are particularly well-suited for the beauty and fashion industries, where consumers are increasingly using AR and VR to try on products before making a purchase.

Artificial intelligence (AI) is also becoming more prevalent in influencer marketing. AI can be used to analyze data and identify trends, which can help brands to identify the most effective influencers for their campaigns. AI can also be used to create more personalized content for individual consumers, which can increase engagement and loyalty.

Overall, the future of influencer marketing is likely to be shaped by these emerging trends and technologies. Brands and influencers will need to stay up-to-date with these developments in order to remain competitive and successful in the industry.

As the influencer marketing industry continues to evolve and adapt to new technologies and trends, it is important for influencers to stay ahead of the curve and be prepared for the changes that lie ahead. Here are some practical tips for influencers to consider:

1. Stay informed: One of the most important things that influencers can do to stay ahead of the curve is to stay informed

about industry trends and emerging technologies. This means staying up-to-date on news and developments in the influencer marketing industry, attending industry conferences and events, and following thought leaders and influencers on social media.

2. Experiment with new platforms and formats: As new social media platforms and content formats emerge, it is important for influencers to experiment with these new tools in order to stay relevant and reach new audiences. Whether it's short-form video content or long-form storytelling, influencers should be open to trying new things and finding new ways to engage their followers.

3. Focus on authenticity: As the influencer marketing industry continues to grow and become more regulated, it is increasingly important for influencers to focus on authenticity in their content and partnerships. This means being transparent about sponsored content, disclosing any financial relationships with brands, and only promoting products and services that align with their personal values and interests.

4. Build relationships with brands: In order to succeed as an influencer, it is important to build strong relationships with brands and marketers. This means networking with industry professionals, attending events and conferences, and reaching out to brands to pitch partnership ideas. Building strong relationships with brands can lead to long-term partnerships and collaborations, which can be key to sustained success as an influencer.

5. Diversify your income streams: As the influencer marketing industry becomes more competitive, it is important for influencers to diversify their income streams and explore other revenue opportunities. This could include selling products or services, creating digital courses or e-books, or working as a consultant or coach.

6. Collaborate with other influencers: Collaborating with other influencers can be a great way to reach new audiences, share expertise, and build relationships within the industry. Whether it's through co-creating content, guest posting on each other's

blogs, or hosting joint events or webinars, collaborating with other influencers can help to expand your reach and build your personal brand.

7. Focus on long-term growth: Finally, it is important for influencers to focus on long-term growth and sustainability, rather than short-term gains. This means prioritizing quality over quantity, building strong relationships with followers and brands, and investing time and resources into building a strong personal brand and online presence. By focusing on long-term growth, influencers can build a sustainable and successful career in the influencer marketing industry.

Influencer marketing has revolutionized the way businesses connect with consumers, and the industry shows no signs of slowing down. From micro-influencers to celebrity influencers, there are endless possibilities for brands to leverage the power of social media to reach their target audiences. However, with this power comes responsibility, and influencers must navigate the challenges and pitfalls of the industry to achieve long-term success.

In this chapter, we have explored the evolution of influencer marketing, the importance of building a personal brand, and the strategies used by successful influencers to grow their following. We have also discussed the challenges and pitfalls of working as an influencer, including the impact of sponsored content and the need for authenticity, as well as the legal and ethical considerations of the industry.

As the industry continues to evolve, it is important for influencers to stay ahead of the curve and adapt to emerging trends and technologies. This means continually innovating and finding new ways to connect with audiences while maintaining transparency and authenticity.

One emerging trend is the rise of virtual influencers, which are computer-generated characters that can promote products and services on social media. These virtual influencers have already gained traction with brands and could become a significant part of the influencer marketing landscape in the coming years.

Another trend is the increasing use of data analytics and artificial intelligence (AI) in influencer marketing. This technology can help brands identify the right influencers to work with and predict the success of campaigns, making it easier for them to make informed decisions and achieve better results.

Influencer marketing is an exciting and dynamic industry, but it is important for influencers to approach it with a clear understanding of the challenges and opportunities that come with it. By building a strong personal brand, maintaining authenticity, and staying ahead of emerging trends and technologies, influencers can navigate the business of influencing and achieve long-term success.

In conclusion, the future of influencer marketing is bright, and there is no doubt that it will continue to shape the way businesses connect with consumers. As the industry evolves, it is important for influencers to stay true to their values and maintain authenticity while embracing new technologies and finding new ways to connect with their audiences. With the right strategies and a commitment to ethical and legal standards, influencers can thrive in this exciting and ever-changing industry.

Navigating the Online Marketplace

The rise of the internet and social media has transformed the way we do business, and the online marketplace has become a powerful tool for entrepreneurs and businesses of all sizes to reach new customers and expand their reach. However, navigating the complexities of the online marketplace can be challenging, and success often requires a combination of strategic thinking, creativity, and a deep understanding of the digital landscape.

In this chapter, we will explore the many opportunities and challenges of the online marketplace, and provide practical advice for businesses and entrepreneurs who are looking to establish or grow their online presence. We will examine the various channels and platforms available for reaching customers online, and discuss the best practices and strategies for effectively engaging with audiences in the digital age.

At the same time, we will also explore the many challenges and pitfalls of the online marketplace, from fierce competition and rapidly changing consumer trends to issues of online safety and privacy. We will examine the risks and benefits of various online business models, and discuss the importance of maintaining a strong ethical and legal framework in the pursuit of online success.

Whether you are a seasoned entrepreneur or a newcomer to the world of online business, this chapter will provide valuable insights and practical strategies for navigating the ever-changing digital landscape and thriving in the online marketplace. So let us dive in and explore the exciting opportunities and challenges of the online world.

The Benefits and Challenges of Online Marketplaces:

As the internet has grown and evolved over the past few decades, so too have the opportunities for entrepreneurs and businesses to reach a global audience through online marketplaces. These platforms have opened up new avenues for small businesses and independent sellers to sell their products and services to a massive customer base.

However, along with the benefits of online marketplaces come unique challenges and considerations. In this section, we will explore both the benefits and challenges of selling on online marketplaces and provide practical advice for navigating this competitive and constantly evolving landscape.

In recent years, online marketplaces have become increasingly popular for businesses of all sizes. From small startups to large corporations, online marketplaces offer a number of benefits that traditional brick-and-mortar stores simply cannot match. One of the biggest advantages of online marketplaces is increased visibility. By listing products on popular marketplaces, businesses can reach a wider audience of potential customers than they would through a physical storefront alone.

Online marketplaces also provide access to a larger customer base, as consumers can shop from anywhere in the world with just a few clicks. This can be particularly advantageous for businesses that specialize in niche products or services, as it allows them to find customers who might not be located in their local area. Additionally, online marketplaces often provide businesses with tools to track and analyze customer data, allowing them to better understand their target audience and make more informed decisions about their marketing and sales strategies.

Another major benefit of online marketplaces is the reduced overhead costs compared to traditional brick-and-mortar stores. By selling products online, businesses can avoid the costs associated with maintaining a physical storefront, such as rent, utilities, and staffing. This can be particularly advantageous for small businesses or entrepreneurs who may not have the resources to open a physical store.

Despite these benefits, however, there are also several challenges associated with selling on online marketplaces. One of the biggest challenges is competition. With so many businesses selling similar products or services on these platforms, it can be difficult to stand out and attract customers. Additionally, online marketplaces often take a commission on sales, which can eat into a business's profit margins.

Another challenge is the potential for counterfeit or fraudulent products. As online marketplaces become more popular, they also become a target for scammers and counterfeiters looking to take advantage of unsuspecting customers. This can not only harm the reputation of the marketplace, but also the reputation of the businesses selling on the platform.

While there are certainly challenges associated with selling on online marketplaces, the benefits they offer are often too great to ignore. In the following sections, we will explore some of the most popular online marketplaces and discuss the strategies businesses can use to succeed in these competitive and ever-evolving marketplaces.

Online marketplaces have become increasingly popular in recent years, as businesses seek to expand their reach and tap into a wider customer base. While these platforms offer many benefits, such as increased visibility and reduced overhead costs, they also present a number of challenges that businesses must navigate in order to succeed.

One of the primary challenges of online marketplaces is the increased competition that businesses face. With so many sellers offering similar products or services, it can be difficult for businesses to stand out and capture the attention of potential customers. This is especially true in crowded marketplaces, where businesses must compete with hundreds or even thousands of other sellers.

Another challenge of online marketplaces is the need for strong branding. With so many options available to consumers, it's important for businesses to differentiate themselves and establish a clear brand identity. This includes developing a strong logo, messaging, and visual style that resonates with customers and sets the business apart from its competitors.

Negative reviews and customer feedback can also be a significant challenge for businesses operating in online marketplaces. With the ability for customers to easily leave feedback and ratings, businesses must work hard to maintain a positive reputation and address any negative comments or complaints. This requires a strong commitment to customer service and the ability to respond quickly and effectively to customer concerns.

Despite these challenges, online marketplaces offer many benefits to businesses looking to expand their reach and grow their customer base. By leveraging the power of these platforms, businesses can reach a wider audience and tap into new markets, while also reducing overhead costs and improving efficiency.

In order to succeed in online marketplaces, businesses must develop a clear strategy for standing out in a crowded marketplace, establishing a strong brand identity, and maintaining a positive reputation with customers. This requires a deep understanding of the unique challenges and opportunities of online marketplaces, as well as a commitment to continuous improvement and adaptation to changing market conditions.

As online marketplaces continue to evolve and grow, businesses must stay ahead of the curve and adapt to new trends and technologies in order to remain competitive and achieve long-term success. This requires a combination of strategic planning, careful execution, and a commitment to ongoing innovation and improvement.

Building a Successful Online Presence

The online marketplace is a highly competitive space, where businesses need to establish a strong online presence to stay ahead of the competition. In today's digital age, having a strong online presence is crucial for businesses of all sizes, whether they operate solely online or have a physical storefront. This section will focus on the key strategies businesses can use to build a successful online presence, including creating a strong brand identity, building an engaging website, and leveraging social media and other digital marketing channels.

In the world of online marketplaces, a strong online presence is essential for businesses looking to succeed. In today's digital age, customers increasingly turn to the internet to research products, read reviews, and make purchases. As a result, businesses that fail to establish a strong online presence risk getting left behind by their competitors.

One of the key benefits of a strong online presence is increased visibility. By creating a website, social media profiles, and other online channels, businesses can reach a wider audience than they could through traditional marketing methods alone. A strong online presence can also help to build brand awareness, as customers become more familiar with a business's name, logo, and products.

Another benefit of a strong online presence is the ability to engage with customers on a more personal level. Social media platforms, for example, allow businesses to interact directly with customers, answering questions, addressing concerns, and providing personalized recommendations. This level of engagement can help to build customer loyalty and trust, ultimately leading to increased sales and revenue.

However, building a strong online presence also comes with its challenges. With so many businesses vying for attention online, it can be difficult to stand out from the crowd. It is essential for businesses to establish a strong brand identity, which includes creating a unique logo, choosing a distinct color scheme, and crafting a compelling brand message.

Another challenge of building a strong online presence is the need to stay up-to-date with the latest trends and technologies. With new platforms and features emerging all the time, businesses must be able to adapt quickly and effectively. This requires a willingness to experiment with new tools and techniques, as well as a commitment to ongoing learning and professional development.

In addition to these challenges, businesses operating in the online marketplace also face the potential for negative reviews and customer feedback. While it is impossible to please every customer all the time, businesses must be prepared to handle negative feedback in a professional and proactive manner. This may involve responding to negative reviews, offering refunds or exchanges, or providing additional support to customers who have had a negative experience.

Overall, a strong online presence is essential for businesses operating in the online marketplace. While it comes with its challenges, the benefits of increased visibility, engagement, and customer loyalty make it well worth the effort.

As businesses move into the online marketplace, building a strong online presence becomes increasingly important. An effective online presence can help businesses to increase visibility, attract new customers, and build brand loyalty. In today's digital age, having a strong online presence is no longer a luxury, but a necessity.

The elements of a successful online presence vary depending on the business and the industry, but there are some general principles that can be applied across the board. One of the most important elements of a successful online presence is a well-designed website. A website is often the first point of contact that potential customers have with a business, and it's important that the website be visually appealing, easy to navigate, and provide all the necessary information about the business's products or services.

Another important element of a successful online presence is a strong social media presence. Social media platforms provide businesses with an opportunity to connect with customers in a more informal, conversational way. By posting regular updates, engaging with customers, and sharing interesting and relevant content, businesses can build a loyal following on social media.

Engaging content is another important element of a successful online presence. Whether it's blog posts, videos, or infographics, creating content that is interesting, informative, and relevant to the target audience can help businesses to establish themselves as thought leaders in their industry and build trust with potential customers.

Search engine optimization (SEO) is also an important element of a successful online presence. By optimizing their website and content for search engines, businesses can increase their visibility and attract more organic traffic to their site. This can be achieved through tactics such as keyword research, link building, and creating high-quality, shareable content.

Finally, building a successful online presence requires a commitment to ongoing improvement and optimization. This involves regularly analyzing website traffic, social media engagement, and other metrics to identify areas for improvement and make necessary adjustments.

In summary, building a successful online presence involves a combination of a well-designed website, a strong social media presence, engaging content, effective SEO, and ongoing analysis and optimization. By prioritizing these elements, businesses can establish themselves as leaders in their industry and attract a loyal following of customers.

As businesses continue to operate in the online marketplace, it is becoming increasingly important to establish and maintain a strong online presence. An online presence can help businesses build brand recognition, reach new customers, and increase sales. However, with so many options and channels available, it can be challenging for businesses to know where to start. In this section, we will explore the elements of a successful online presence and provide practical advice for businesses on how to build and maintain it.

1. Develop a Strong Brand Identity: Your brand identity is how you want your business to be perceived by the world. It includes elements such as your logo, color scheme, tone of voice, and messaging. Developing a strong brand identity is critical to building a successful online presence. It will help you stand out from the competition and make a lasting impression on potential customers.

2. Create a Professional Website: Your website is the foundation of your online presence. It is where potential customers will go to learn more about your business, products, and services. A professional website should be visually appealing, easy to navigate, and mobile-friendly. It should also have clear calls to action, such as a sign-up form or a purchase button.

3. Optimize for Search Engines: Search engine optimization (SEO) is the process of optimizing your website to rank higher in search engine results pages. By optimizing your website, you can increase visibility and attract more traffic to your site. Some key SEO tactics include using relevant keywords, creating high-quality content, and building quality backlinks to your site.

4. Engage on Social Media: Social media platforms provide businesses with an opportunity to connect with customers and build brand awareness. When creating your social media strategy, focus on platforms that your target audience uses the most. Create engaging content that aligns with your brand, and don't be afraid to experiment with different types of content, such as images, videos, and infographics.

5. Use Email Marketing: Email marketing is a powerful tool for businesses looking to build and maintain relationships with customers. Create a targeted email list and send out regular newsletters and promotions to keep your audience engaged. Be sure to personalize your messages and include a clear call to action.

6. Monitor and Respond to Reviews: Online reviews can have a significant impact on a business's reputation. Make sure to monitor reviews on platforms, and social media. Respond promptly and professionally to both positive and negative reviews, as this can help build trust with customers.

7. Continuously Analyze and Improve: Building a strong online presence is an ongoing process. It's important to continuously analyze and improve your online presence based on the data and feedback you receive. Use analytics tools to track website traffic, social media engagement, and email open rates. Use this data to make informed decisions and adjust your strategy as needed.

Building a successful online presence requires a thoughtful and strategic approach. By developing a strong brand identity, creating a professional website, optimizing for search engines, engaging on social media, using email marketing, monitoring and responding to reviews, and continuously analyzing and improving, businesses can establish a strong online presence that attracts and retains customers.

Strategies for Standing Out in the Online Marketplace

In the highly competitive world of online marketplaces, businesses need to be strategic in order to stand out and succeed. With millions of products and services available at consumers' fingertips, it can be challenging for businesses to differentiate themselves from their competitors. In this section, we will explore some effective strategies for businesses to stand out in the online marketplace and attract and retain customers. We will analyze the importance of branding, pricing, customer service, and other factors that can make a significant impact on a business's success in the online marketplace. By implementing these strategies, businesses can increase their visibility, build customer loyalty, and ultimately grow their bottom line.

In today's digital age, competition in the online marketplace is fierce. With the ease of access to technology, it has become simpler than ever for businesses to set up shop online, but it also means that there is a higher volume of competition in the space. For businesses to succeed in the online marketplace, it's essential to differentiate themselves and stand out from the crowd.

There are several strategies that businesses can use to differentiate themselves and stand out in the online marketplace. One such strategy is to focus on building a strong brand identity. Brands that have a clear and consistent message, logo, and overall visual aesthetic are more likely to be remembered and recognized by consumers. This means investing in professional branding and design, creating a strong social media presence, and maintaining a consistent voice and tone in all communications.

Another strategy for standing out in the online marketplace is to offer exceptional customer service. In today's digital age, consumers expect quick and personalized service, and businesses that can deliver on this expectation will be more likely to succeed. This means investing in customer service training for employees, using chatbots or other digital tools to provide quick and efficient service, and responding promptly and professionally to customer feedback and reviews.

In addition to building a strong brand identity and offering exceptional customer service, businesses can differentiate themselves by offering unique and innovative products or services. This means staying up-to-date with trends and market research, and constantly innovating and iterating to provide customers with something new and exciting.

Another strategy for standing out in the online marketplace is to create compelling content that engages and informs customers. This can include blog posts, videos, social media posts, and other types of content that provide value to customers and showcase the business's expertise and knowledge in their industry.

Finally, businesses can differentiate themselves by offering competitive pricing and promotions. This means staying up-to-date with industry pricing trends and offering discounts or promotions that are competitive and attractive to customers.

In today's crowded online marketplace, it's more important than ever for businesses to differentiate themselves from their competitors. This requires developing a unique value proposition, building a strong brand, and delivering exceptional customer service.

A value proposition is a statement that explains what makes a product or service unique and valuable to customers. A strong value proposition can help businesses stand out in a crowded market by highlighting the benefits of their products or services and differentiating themselves from their competitors. For example, a company that sells organic skincare products might have a value proposition that emphasizes the natural ingredients used in their products and the benefits they provide for the skin.

Building a strong brand is also critical for businesses looking to stand out in the online marketplace. A brand is more than just a logo or a tagline – it's the overall perception that customers have of a company.

A strong brand can help businesses create a memorable identity and build trust with their customers. This can be achieved through consistent messaging, a well-designed website and social media presence, and a focus on creating a positive customer experience.

Exceptional customer service is another key factor in standing out in the online marketplace. In a world where customers have endless options, providing a great customer experience can be the difference between success and failure. This includes things like responding promptly to customer inquiries, providing accurate product information, and resolving any issues or complaints in a timely and professional manner.

In addition to these core strategies, businesses can also stand out by offering unique product offerings, creating engaging content and social media campaigns, and leveraging the power of influencer marketing. For example, a company that sells handmade pottery might offer personalized customization options that are not available from other retailers. Or a clothing brand might create a social media campaign that highlights the stories of real customers and how the brand has impacted their lives.

Ultimately, standing out in the online marketplace requires a combination of strategic planning, effective execution, and a relentless focus on delivering value to customers. By developing a strong value proposition, building a memorable brand, providing exceptional customer service, and leveraging unique strategies, businesses can differentiate themselves from their competitors and succeed in today's crowded online marketplace.

As the online marketplace becomes increasingly crowded, it is more important than ever for businesses to differentiate themselves and stand out from the competition. In this section, we will discuss practical strategies that businesses can use to achieve this goal.

1. Develop a unique value proposition One of the most effective ways to stand out in the online marketplace is to develop a

unique value proposition. A value proposition is a statement that explains why customers should choose your product or service over those of your competitors. It should be clear, concise, and focused on the specific benefits that your product or service offers to customers. A strong value proposition can help to differentiate your business from the competition and attract more customers.

2. To develop a unique value proposition, businesses should start by conducting market research to understand the needs and preferences of their target audience. This research should be used to identify gaps in the market that the business can fill with a unique product or service. Once the value proposition has been developed, it should be prominently displayed on the business's website and other marketing materials.

3. Build a strong brand Effective branding is another key strategy for standing out in the online marketplace. A strong brand can help to establish trust and credibility with customers, and make your business more memorable and recognizable. A strong brand should include a clear and consistent message, a distinctive visual identity, and a strong online presence.

4. To build a strong brand, businesses should start by defining their brand identity, including their mission, values, and personality. This identity should be reflected in all aspects of the business, from the website and social media profiles to the packaging and marketing materials. Consistency is key, and all messaging and visual elements should be aligned with the brand identity.

5. Provide exceptional customer service In the online marketplace, customer service is more important than ever. With so many options available, customers are more likely to choose a business that offers exceptional service and support. To stand out from the competition, businesses should prioritize customer service and make it a core part of their brand identity.

6. Exceptional customer service starts with understanding the needs and preferences of your customers. Businesses should listen to customer feedback and make changes to their

products or services accordingly. They should also make it easy for customers to get in touch and offer multiple channels of support, such as email, phone, and chat.

7. Leverage social media Social media is a powerful tool for businesses looking to stand out in the online marketplace. By leveraging social media, businesses can reach a larger audience, engage with customers, and build brand awareness.

8. To effectively leverage social media, businesses should start by identifying the platforms that are most relevant to their target audience. They should then create a content strategy that is tailored to each platform, including a mix of promotional and informational content. Consistency is key, and businesses should post regularly to keep their audience engaged.

9. Offer value-added services Finally, businesses can differentiate themselves by offering value-added services that go above and beyond what their competitors are offering. This could include things like free shipping, personalized recommendations, or exclusive discounts for loyal customers. By offering these types of services, businesses can create a sense of loyalty and trust with their customers, and increase the likelihood of repeat business.

Standing out in the online marketplace is challenging, but it is not impossible. By developing a unique value proposition, building a strong brand, providing exceptional customer service, leveraging social media, and offering value-added services, businesses can differentiate themselves and attract more customers. The key is to understand the needs and preferences of your target audience, and tailor your strategies accordingly.

Navigating Online Advertising and Marketing

In today's digital age, online advertising and marketing play a critical role in the success of businesses operating in the online marketplace. From paid search advertising to social media marketing, there are a wide variety of strategies and tactics available for businesses to reach and engage their target audience. However, with so many options available, navigating the world of online advertising and marketing can be a challenge. In this section, we will explore the benefits and challenges of online advertising and marketing, as well as provide practical advice for businesses looking to effectively promote their products or services online.

In today's digital age, online advertising and marketing play a crucial role in the success of businesses operating in the online marketplace. With billions of internet users worldwide, businesses have the opportunity to reach a vast audience through various online channels, including social media, search engines, and display advertising.

One of the primary benefits of online advertising and marketing is the ability to target specific audiences. Through data analysis and targeting tools, businesses can tailor their advertising and marketing efforts to reach the individuals most likely to be interested in their products or services. This targeted approach can lead to increased conversions and ultimately, a higher return on investment (ROI).

Another benefit of online advertising and marketing is the ability to measure and track results. Unlike traditional advertising methods, such as print or television ads, businesses can track the performance of their online advertising and marketing efforts in real-time. This allows them to adjust their strategies as needed to optimize their ROI.

However, online advertising and marketing also come with their challenges. One of the most significant challenges is the competition for attention. With so many businesses vying for consumers' attention online, it can be challenging to stand out and make an impact. This is why it is crucial for businesses to have a strong brand and unique value proposition.

Another challenge is the potential for negative feedback or reviews. In today's age of social media, one negative review or post can quickly spread and damage a business's reputation. This highlights the importance of exceptional customer service and the need for businesses to address negative feedback promptly and professionally.

In addition to these challenges, businesses must also navigate the ever-changing landscape of online advertising and marketing. With new technologies and trends emerging regularly, businesses must stay up-to-date and adapt their strategies to remain effective.

Overall, online advertising and marketing play a crucial role in the success of businesses operating in the online marketplace. While there are challenges to navigate, the benefits of targeted advertising, measurable results, and the ability to reach a vast audience make it a valuable tool for businesses looking to grow and succeed in the digital age.

Online advertising and marketing play a significant role in the online marketplace. With the rise of e-commerce and the increasing number of businesses entering the digital space, it has become crucial for businesses to have a strong online presence and promote their products and services through various digital channels.

One of the primary benefits of online advertising is its targeting capabilities. Unlike traditional advertising, digital advertising allows businesses to reach their target audience more effectively by using various targeting parameters such as age, gender, interests, and location. This enables businesses to deliver their message to the right audience, increasing the likelihood of conversions and sales.

However, with the growing number of online ads, ad fatigue has become a challenge for businesses. Consumers are inundated with ads across multiple digital platforms, leading to a decline in their effectiveness. This has led businesses to focus on creating more engaging and interactive ad formats such as video ads, interactive ads, and sponsored content to capture the attention of their target audience.

Another challenge of online advertising is the rise of ad-blockers. Ad-blockers are software tools that prevent ads from being displayed on a user's device, making it difficult for businesses to reach their target audience. This has led to the need for businesses to create nonintrusive ads that add value to the user experience, making it less likely for them to use ad-blockers.

In addition to online advertising, online marketing also plays a significant role in the online marketplace. Online marketing includes various digital channels such as social media marketing, email marketing, search engine optimization (SEO), and content marketing.

Social media marketing involves promoting products or services through social media platforms. Social media platforms provide businesses with an opportunity to connect with their target audience, build brand awareness, and drive conversions. However, with the increasing competition and changes in algorithms, it has become crucial for businesses to create engaging content and use paid social media advertising to reach their target audience effectively.

Email marketing involves sending promotional emails to a list of subscribers to promote products or services. Email marketing allows businesses to communicate directly with their audience, providing them with personalized content and offers. However, with the rise of spam emails, businesses need to ensure that their emails provide value to the recipient and comply with data protection regulations such as GDPR.

SEO involves optimizing a website to rank higher on search engine results pages (SERPs). This is done by optimizing the website's content and structure to align with search engine algorithms, making it easier for users to find the website when searching for related keywords. SEO has become a critical aspect of online marketing, as it helps businesses increase their visibility and drive organic traffic to their website.

Content marketing involves creating and sharing valuable and relevant content to attract and retain a target audience. This can include blog posts, videos, infographics, and social media posts. Content marketing allows businesses to build trust and authority with their audience, driving conversions and sales. However, with the increasing amount of content available online, businesses need to ensure that their content stands out by creating high-quality, original content that adds value to their audience.

While there are benefits to using digital advertising and marketing, there are also challenges that businesses must overcome. By understanding the challenges and leveraging the benefits, businesses can effectively promote their products and services and stay ahead in the highly competitive digital landscape.

In today's digital age, online advertising and marketing are critical components of any business strategy. With the vast amount of information and products available on the internet, businesses need to employ effective advertising and marketing strategies to stand out in the crowded online marketplace and reach their target audience. However, with the constantly evolving technology and trends, it can be challenging for businesses to navigate the world of online advertising and marketing.

One of the first steps in effective online advertising and marketing is understanding the different channels available to businesses. These channels can include social media platforms, search engines, email marketing, display ads, and video ads. Each channel has its own strengths and weaknesses, and it's important for businesses to choose the right ones based on their target audience and business goals.

Social media platforms, for example, are excellent for building brand awareness and engaging with customers. There are two of the most popular social media platforms for businesses, with over 3 billion users combined. Businesses can use these platforms to create engaging content, run targeted ads, and interact with customers through comments and messages.

Search engine marketing, on the other hand, is a great way to reach customers who are actively searching for products or services similar to what a business offers. By optimizing their website and running paid search ads on platforms, businesses can increase their visibility in search results and drive traffic to their website.

Email marketing is another effective channel for reaching customers, particularly those who have already expressed interest in a business's products or services. By sending targeted and personalized emails to subscribers, businesses can keep their brand top-of-mind and encourage repeat purchases.

Display ads and video ads are also powerful tools for businesses to consider. Display ads are visual ads that can appear on websites and apps, while video ads are typically short videos that run before or during online content. These types of ads can help businesses increase brand awareness and engagement.

While these channels offer numerous benefits, there are also challenges to consider. For example, with so many businesses advertising online, it can be challenging to stand out and avoid ad fatigue. Consumers are exposed to so many ads each day that they may become numb to them, leading to a decrease in engagement and effectiveness.

Additionally, the use of ad blockers by consumers is on the rise, which can prevent businesses from reaching their target audience. Ad blockers are software tools that block ads from being displayed on websites and apps, making it important for businesses to employ strategies that can work around them.

To navigate these challenges and effectively reach their target audience through online advertising and marketing, businesses can follow several best practices. One of the most important is to create engaging and relevant content that speaks to their target audience. By understanding their audience's pain points and interests, businesses can create content that resonates with them and encourages engagement.

Another best practice is to track and analyze data regularly. By monitoring the performance of their advertising and marketing campaigns, businesses can identify what's working and what's not, and adjust their strategies accordingly. This data can also provide valuable insights into their target audience and help inform future campaigns.

It's also important for businesses to stay up-to-date with the latest trends and technologies in online advertising and marketing. As new channels and tools emerge, businesses that stay ahead of the curve can gain a competitive advantage and better reach their target audience.

In conclusion, online advertising and marketing are essential components of any business strategy in the digital age. By understanding the different channels available, navigating the challenges, and following best practices, businesses can effectively reach their target audience and stand out in the crowded online marketplace.

The Importance of Customer Experience in the Online Marketplace

In today's highly competitive online marketplace, providing an exceptional customer experience has become more important than ever before. As consumers have come to expect personalized, seamless, and convenient interactions with businesses, companies must prioritize customer experience to stay ahead of the competition. In this section, we will explore the significance of customer experience in the online marketplace, analyze the impact it can have on a business's success, and provide practical advice for businesses looking to improve their customer experience.

In today's digital age, consumers have more options than ever before when it comes to purchasing products and services. With just a few clicks, they can compare prices, read reviews, and make purchases from businesses all around the world. As a result, businesses operating in the online marketplace are faced with increased competition, and must work harder than ever to stand out from the crowd.

One key way that businesses can differentiate themselves and build customer loyalty is by delivering a positive customer experience. In fact, research has shown that customers are willing to pay more for a product or service if they believe they will receive a better experience.

The customer experience encompasses all interactions that a customer has with a business, from browsing the website to making a purchase and receiving post-sale support. It's about creating a seamless and enjoyable journey for the customer, and leaving them feeling satisfied and valued.

In the online marketplace, delivering a positive customer experience is essential for businesses looking to succeed. Customers expect a fast, easy, and convenient shopping experience, and are quick to turn to competitors if their expectations are not met.

Furthermore, a positive customer experience can lead to increased customer loyalty, repeat business, and positive word-of-mouth recommendations. On the other hand, a negative customer experience can quickly lead to negative reviews, lost business, and a damaged reputation.

In this section, we will explore the importance of delivering a positive customer experience in the online marketplace, as well as strategies and best practices for achieving this goal. We will also analyze the impact of a positive customer experience on business success and growth.

Customer reviews and feedback have become a crucial part of a business's online reputation. With the abundance of information available at our fingertips, consumers are becoming more and more reliant on the opinions of others before making a purchase decision. In fact, according to a survey conducted by BrightLocal, 91% of consumers read online reviews before making a purchase, and 84% trust online reviews as much as a personal recommendation.

Positive customer reviews can have a significant impact on a business's success in the online marketplace. They can help to increase visibility, build trust and credibility, and drive sales. On the other hand, negative reviews can have the opposite effect, damaging a business's reputation and potentially leading to a loss of customers and revenue.

It's important for businesses to understand the role of customer reviews and feedback in shaping their online reputation and take steps to actively manage it. This involves not only responding to negative reviews in a timely and professional manner, but also proactively seeking out and encouraging positive reviews from satisfied customers.

One effective way to do this is by utilizing online review management tools, such as ReviewTrackers or Podium, which can help businesses monitor and respond to reviews across multiple platforms, as well as automate review requests to customers.

Additionally, businesses should strive to provide a positive customer experience from start to finish, ensuring that their products or services meet or exceed customer expectations. This can be achieved through effective communication, transparent pricing, easy-to-use websites, and responsive customer support.

Ultimately, businesses that prioritize customer experience and actively manage their online reputation through customer reviews and feedback are more likely to succeed in the competitive online marketplace.

In today's highly competitive online marketplace, providing exceptional customer service has become increasingly important. Consumers have numerous options for purchasing products and services online, which means businesses need to go above and beyond to stand out from their competitors. In this section, we will discuss practical advice for businesses on how to deliver exceptional customer service and manage customer feedback.

1. Communicate Clearly and Effectively: One of the most important aspects of providing exceptional customer service is clear and effective communication. Customers should be able

to easily find information about products and services, shipping times, and return policies. Businesses should also provide clear and prompt responses to customer inquiries and complaints.

2. Personalize the Customer Experience: Personalization is key to building a loyal customer base. Businesses should strive to create a personalized experience for each customer, taking into account their individual preferences and needs. This can be achieved through personalized product recommendations, targeted marketing campaigns, and tailored customer service interactions.

3. Offer Multiple Channels for Customer Support: In addition to providing clear and effective communication, businesses should also offer multiple channels for customer support. This includes email, phone, and chat support, as well as social media and self-service options. By offering multiple channels for customer support, businesses can meet the needs of a wider range of customers and improve overall customer satisfaction.

4. Respond to Feedback and Reviews: Customer reviews and feedback can provide valuable insights into what customers like and dislike about a business. Businesses should regularly monitor and respond to customer feedback and reviews, addressing any concerns or complaints in a timely and professional manner. By responding to customer feedback, businesses can improve their reputation and build trust with their customers.

5. Train and Empower Customer Service Representatives: Customer service representatives are on the front lines of a business's customer service efforts. It is important to provide them with the training and resources they need to effectively address customer inquiries and complaints. Businesses should also empower their customer service representatives to make decisions and take actions that will benefit the customer and improve their overall experience.

6. Measure and Monitor Customer Satisfaction: Finally, businesses should regularly measure and monitor customer satisfaction to identify areas for improvement. This can be done through

surveys, customer feedback forms, and other tools. By regularly monitoring customer satisfaction, businesses can identify trends and make strategic changes to improve the customer experience.

Providing exceptional customer service is essential for success in the online marketplace. By communicating clearly and effectively, personalizing the customer experience, offering multiple channels for customer support, responding to feedback and reviews, training and empowering customer service representatives, and measuring and monitoring customer satisfaction, businesses can create a positive and memorable customer experience that sets them apart from their competitors.

Embracing Innovation and Adapting to Change

As the online marketplace continues to evolve and expand, businesses must stay ahead of the curve in order to remain competitive and successful. Embracing innovation and adapting to change are key factors in navigating the ever-changing landscape of the online marketplace. In this section, we will explore the importance of staying up-to-date with the latest trends and technologies, as well as how to effectively implement them into business strategies. Additionally, we will discuss the potential risks and challenges of adopting new technologies and provide practical advice on how to mitigate them. By embracing innovation and adapting to change, businesses can position themselves for long-term success in the online marketplace.

As the online marketplace continues to evolve at a rapid pace, it is becoming increasingly important for businesses to embrace innovation and adapt to changing trends and consumer behavior. This section will explore the significance of these two key factors in the success of businesses operating in the online marketplace.

Innovation is critical for businesses to stay competitive and relevant in a rapidly changing digital landscape. The speed at which technology advances and new trends emerge can be overwhelming for businesses, but it is essential to keep up with these changes to remain relevant to customers. Innovation can take many forms, including new product development, process improvements, and the adoption of new technologies.

Adaptability is another critical factor for success in the online marketplace. With the constantly changing landscape, businesses must be able to adapt to new trends and consumer behaviors quickly. Being able to pivot and adjust strategies to meet the changing needs of customers can be the difference between success and failure in the online marketplace.

In this section, we will explore the importance of innovation and adaptability, and provide practical advice on how businesses can embrace these two factors to succeed in the online marketplace.

The online marketplace is constantly evolving, with emerging trends and technologies shaping the way businesses operate and connect with customers. To stay competitive and successful in this fast-paced environment, it is crucial for businesses to embrace innovation and adapt to change.

One of the most significant emerging trends in the online marketplace is the use of artificial intelligence (AI). AI technology can be used to improve the customer experience by personalizing recommendations, streamlining communication channels, and automating routine tasks. For example, chatbots powered by AI can provide 24/7 customer support, freeing up human agents to handle more complex inquiries.

Voice search is another emerging technology that is rapidly gaining popularity. With the rise of smart speakers and voice assistants, more and more consumers are using voice search to find products and services online. To stay ahead of the curve, businesses must ensure that their websites and content are optimized for voice search.

Other emerging trends in the online marketplace include the growing popularity of video content, the increasing importance of mobile optimization, and the rise of social commerce. Businesses that are able to adapt to these trends and incorporate them into their marketing strategies will have a distinct advantage in the online marketplace.

It is important to note that the pace of innovation in the online marketplace is only accelerating. As such, businesses must remain agile and adaptable in order to keep up with the latest trends and technologies. This requires a willingness to experiment and take risks, as well as a commitment to ongoing learning and professional development.

In addition to embracing innovation, businesses must also be prepared to adapt to changing consumer behaviors and preferences. This requires a deep understanding of the target audience and a willingness to pivot strategies as needed. For example, if a particular marketing campaign or product offering is not resonating with consumers, businesses must be willing to adjust their approach in order to meet changing needs and preferences.

Ultimately, businesses that are able to embrace innovation and adapt to change will be well-positioned to succeed in the fast-paced and constantly evolving online marketplace. This requires a commitment to ongoing learning and professional development, as well as a willingness to experiment and take risks in pursuit of new opportunities.

The world of online commerce is constantly evolving, and businesses that fail to keep up with the latest trends and technologies risk falling behind their competitors. In today's rapidly changing online marketplace, it's not enough to simply have a website and an online presence; businesses must continually adapt and innovate to stay ahead of the curve.

To embrace innovation and adapt to change, businesses must be willing to experiment with new technologies and strategies, and be open to feedback and constructive criticism. It's important to have a growth mindset and a willingness to learn, and to be proactive in seeking out new opportunities for growth and development.

One of the key trends shaping the future of the online marketplace is the increasing use of artificial intelligence (AI) and machine learning. AI is already being used in a variety of ways in the e-commerce world, from chatbots and virtual assistants that can help customers find what they're looking for, to predictive analytics tools that can help businesses anticipate customer needs and preferences.

Another emerging trend is the rise of voice search and smart speakers, which are changing the way people interact with online content and search for products and services. Businesses that want to stay ahead of the curve in this area will need to optimize their content for voice search and ensure that their products and services are easily discoverable through voice-enabled devices.

Other key trends to watch in the online marketplace include the growing importance of mobile optimization, the increasing popularity of video content, and the rise of social commerce, which allows businesses to sell products directly through social media platforms.

To embrace innovation and adapt to these changing trends, businesses should focus on developing a culture of experimentation and learning. This means being willing to take risks and try new things, while also being open to feedback and constructive criticism. It's also important to stay up-to-date with the latest trends and technologies in the online marketplace, and to seek out opportunities for collaboration and partnership with other businesses in the industry.

One of the best ways to embrace innovation and adapt to change is to invest in ongoing education and training. This can include attending industry conferences and events, taking online courses, or working with outside consultants and experts to stay up-to-date with the latest trends and best practices in the online marketplace.

In addition to embracing innovation, businesses must also be adaptable in the face of change. This means being willing to pivot and adjust course when necessary, and being able to quickly respond to new opportunities or challenges that arise in the online marketplace.

One way to build adaptability into your business is to adopt an agile approach to project management and decision-making. This means breaking down projects into smaller, more manageable tasks, and using data and feedback to make decisions and course correct as needed.

Another key to adaptability is being willing to learn from failure. In the fast-paced world of online commerce, businesses will inevitably experience setbacks and failures along the way. The key is to view these failures as opportunities for growth and learning, and to use them as a stepping stone to future success.

One successful case study in the online marketplace is the story of Warby Parker, an eyewear company that disrupted the traditional retail model with a direct-to-consumer approach.

Warby Parker was founded in 2010 by four friends who were frustrated with the high cost of eyewear and the limited options available to consumers. They saw an opportunity to offer stylish, affordable glasses online and began building their business.

To differentiate themselves from other online eyewear retailers, Warby Parker focused on providing exceptional customer service and a unique brand experience. They offered free home try-ons, where customers could select five pairs of glasses to try on at home before making a purchase. They also created a social mission, partnering with non-profits to provide glasses to those in need.

Warby Parker's approach was a hit with consumers, and the company quickly gained a loyal following. Their innovative model and strong branding led to significant growth, with the company reaching $1 billion in valuation in just seven years.

However, Warby Parker has also faced challenges as they have grown. The company has had to navigate changes in the online marketplace, including increased competition and evolving consumer preferences. They have responded by continuing to innovate and experiment with new technologies, such as using augmented reality to allow customers to virtually try on glasses.

Overall, Warby Parker's success can be attributed to their focus on providing a unique customer experience, strong branding, and their ability to adapt to changes in the marketplace. Their story serves as a valuable lesson for businesses looking to succeed in the online marketplace by prioritizing innovation, differentiation, and customer experience.

Embracing innovation and adapting to change are essential for success in the fast-paced and ever-changing online marketplace. By staying up-to-date with the latest trends and technologies, investing in ongoing education and training, and building a culture of experimentation and adaptability, businesses can stay ahead of the curve and thrive in the competitive world of online commerce.

Vlogging and Short Video Platforms

The rise of video content has revolutionized the online world, with vlogging and short video platforms becoming increasingly popular among audiences and content creators alike. From video platforms, these platforms offer a unique opportunity for businesses and individuals to engage with their audience in an authentic and visually compelling way.

In this chapter, we will explore the world of vlogging and short video platforms, and analyze their impact on the online marketplace. We will examine the benefits and challenges of using these platforms for businesses and influencers, and provide practical advice on how to leverage these platforms to build a successful online presence.

From the growth of video platforms as a content creation platform to the explosive rise of short video platforms, we will analyze the evolution of vlogging and short video platforms and their impact on the online marketplace. We will explore the unique advantages that these platforms offer for businesses and influencers, and examine the challenges of producing high-quality video content that resonates with audiences.

With the growing importance of video content in the online world, it is essential for businesses and influencers to understand the opportunities and challenges presented by these platforms. By mastering the art of vlogging and short video content, brands and individuals can create a loyal following and connect with audiences in a way that is both engaging and impactful.

The history of vlogging and short video platforms can be traced back to the early 2000s when the first video blogs (vlogs) were created. These vlogs were typically personal and intimate, featuring individuals sharing their daily lives and experiences. However, with the rise of these platforms and social media, vlogging has evolved into a powerful tool for businesses and influencers to connect with their audiences and promote their brands.

Short video platforms, have become increasingly popular in recent years, offering a quick and easy way to create and share engaging content with a wider audience. These platforms have disrupted the traditional marketing landscape by allowing businesses to reach younger demographics in a more authentic and engaging way.

The impact of vlogging and short video platforms on the online marketplace cannot be overstated. These platforms have provided businesses with new opportunities to connect with customers and promote their products in innovative ways. They have also given rise to a new generation of influencers and content creators, who are leveraging the power of video to build loyal followings and establish themselves as industry leaders.

However, with the benefits of vlogging and short video platforms also come challenges. The competition is fierce, and businesses must constantly adapt and evolve to stay relevant and successful. Additionally, maintaining authenticity and credibility in a landscape where influencers are often paid to promote products is crucial to maintaining a positive reputation and building trust with audiences.

Overall, vlogging and short video platforms have revolutionized the way businesses and influencers approach marketing and brand building. In this chapter, we will explore the evolution of these platforms, their impact on the online marketplace, and provide practical advice for businesses and influencers looking to leverage their power to grow their brands and reach new audiences.

The Rise of Vlogging:

In recent years, vlogging has become a popular and lucrative form of content creation on the internet. Vlogging, or video blogging, involves creating and publishing video content on a regular basis, typically centered around a particular theme or topic. With the rise of sych platforms, more and more people are turning to vlogging as a way to share their experiences, expertise, and personalities with a global audience.

The impact of vlogging on the online marketplace cannot be overstated. Not only do vloggers have the potential to reach large audiences and influence consumer behavior, but they also have the ability to monetize their content through advertising and sponsorships. As such, vlogging has become an important component of many businesses' marketing strategies, as they seek to leverage the power of online influencers to promote their products and services.

In this section, we will explore the rise of vlogging and its impact on the online marketplace. We will discuss the benefits and challenges of vlogging, as well as the strategies used by successful vloggers to grow their audiences and monetize their content. Additionally, we will analyze the evolving landscape of short-form video platforms and their impact on vlogging and the online marketplace.

Vlogging, short for "video blogging," is a type of content creation that involves recording and publishing videos of oneself online, typically on video platforms. The concept of vlogging originated from the concept of blogging, which involves writing and sharing personal stories, experiences, and opinions online through a blog. However, vlogging takes this idea to the next level by using video as the primary medium of communication.

Vlogs can cover a wide range of topics, including personal anecdotes, travel experiences, product reviews, tutorials, and more. The popularity of vlogging has exploded in recent years, with more and more people turning to this form of content creation to share their stories, showcase their talents, and build online communities. In fact, many successful video creators and social media influencers started as vloggers, using their unique perspectives and personalities to attract a loyal following.

The rise of vlogging has also had a significant impact on the online marketplace. Brands are now recognizing the power of influencer marketing through vloggers, who can reach large and engaged audiences through their videos. This has led to the rise of sponsored content and brand collaborations within the vlogging world. Overall, vlogging has become an important aspect of the online ecosystem and is here to stay.

Vlogging, or video blogging, has been steadily growing in popularity since its inception in the early 2000s. It has become a ubiquitous part of online culture, with individuals and businesses alike using the platform to connect with audiences, share experiences, and market products and services.

The rise of vlogging can be attributed to several factors. First, advancements in technology have made it easier and more affordable to produce high-quality videos. With the prevalence of smartphones and affordable cameras, anyone can become a vlogger with minimal investment in equipment.

Second, social media platforms have made it easier to share and promote vlogs, allowing them to reach a wider audience. Some video platforms, in particular, has become the go-to platform for vloggers, with many building large followings and even turning their vlogging hobby into a full-time career.

The impact of vlogging on online culture has been significant. Vloggers have become influencers and thought leaders, with many developing loyal fan bases who follow their every move. The rise of vlogging has also led to a blurring of the lines between personal and professional lives, with many vloggers sharing intimate details of their lives and using their personal brand to promote products and services.

In addition, vlogging has given rise to a new form of entertainment and media consumption. People now turn to vlogs for everything from beauty tutorials to travel advice to political commentary. Vlogging has also provided a platform for underrepresented voices and allowed for diverse perspectives to be shared and amplified.

The rise of vlogging has created numerous success stories for individuals who have developed a strong presence on video platforms. These individuals, known as vloggers, have built dedicated audiences who follow their daily lives, travel adventures, beauty routines, and other interests. The influence of vloggers has also extended to the business world, with many companies partnering with popular vloggers to promote their products and services.

One example of a successful vlogger is Zoella. Zoella began vlogging in 2009 and has since amassed over 11 million subscribers on social media. She has also expanded her brand to include a successful beauty line, books, and collaborations with major brands like Topshop and Pandora. Zoella's influence on her audience has made her a sought-after partner for brands looking to reach young women.

In addition to these individual success stories, the impact of vlogging on the business world has been significant. Many companies have recognized the power of vloggers to influence their audience and have partnered with them to promote their products and services. This has led to the rise of influencer marketing, where businesses pay vloggers to promote their products to their audience.

Overall, the success stories of vloggers and their impact on businesses demonstrate the power of influencer marketing and the importance of building a strong online presence. Vlogging has created a new type of celebrity and a new way for businesses to connect with their audience. As the popularity of vlogging continues to grow, it is likely that we will see more successful partnerships between vloggers and businesses in the future.

The Emergence of Short Video Platforms:

Over the last few years, short video platforms have taken the world by storm, offering users a new and exciting way to consume content. These platforms, have changed the way people create and share videos online, making it easier than ever for businesses to connect with their target audiences in a fun and engaging way. In this section, we will explore the emergence of short video platforms, their impact on the online marketplace, and how businesses can leverage them to reach new customers and build their brand.

Short video platforms refer to social media platforms that allow users to create and share short-form video content. These platforms have gained immense popularity in recent years and have become an integral part of the online marketplace. Some of the most popular short video platforms. These platforms have revolutionized the way users consume and engage with video content, creating new opportunities for businesses and influencers to reach their target audience. In this section, we will explore the emergence of short video platforms and their impact on the online marketplace.

In recent years, short video platforms have taken the internet by storm. These platforms allow users to create and share videos that are typically 60 seconds or less, and they have quickly become some of the most popular social media apps among young people.

Short video platforms experienced explosive growth since its launch in 2016. As of 2021, the app has over 1 billion monthly active users worldwide, and it has been downloaded more than 2 billion times.

Similarly, Reels, which was launched in 2020, has quickly gained popularity and is now a major player in the short video space.

The success of these platforms can be attributed to a few key factors. First, the short video format is highly engaging and allows for quick, easy consumption of content. Second, the platforms use sophisticated algorithms to recommend content to users based on their interests, which helps to keep them engaged and coming back for more. Finally, the platforms have also made it easy for users to create and share their own content, which has led to a proliferation of user-generated content that has helped to fuel their growth.

The rise of short video platforms has had a significant impact on online culture, particularly among younger generations. They have changed the way people consume and create content, and they have also given rise to a new generation of influencers and content creators who have built massive followings on these platforms. As such, they have become an important part of the online marketplace, with businesses and marketers looking to leverage their reach and influence to promote their products and services.

Short video platforms have had a significant impact on online marketing and advertising. With the rise of platforms, businesses are finding new ways to reach their target audience in a more engaging and interactive way.

One of the key advantages of short video platforms is their ability to reach a large and diverse audience. The short and easily consumable format of these videos makes them appealing to a wide range of viewers, particularly younger demographics who are more likely to engage with this type of content.

Short video platforms also provide businesses with a new way to showcase their products and services. Rather than relying on traditional forms of advertising, such as static images or text, businesses can now create engaging and entertaining videos that show their products in action or highlight the benefits of their services.

Another advantage of short video platforms is their ability to encourage user-generated content. With features like challenges and duets, users are encouraged to create their own videos that incorporate a business's products or services. This not only helps to increase engagement with the brand, but also provides businesses with a steady stream of user-generated content that can be shared across their social media channels.

However, there are also challenges associated with using short video platforms for marketing and advertising. One of the biggest challenges is the need to create high-quality, engaging content that resonates with the target audience. With so much competition on these platforms, businesses must find ways to stand out and capture the attention of viewers in a matter of seconds.

Another challenge is the need to stay up-to-date with the constantly evolving features and trends on these platforms. With new features and trends emerging all the time, businesses must be agile and adaptable in their approach to using short video platforms for marketing and advertising.

Despite these challenges, the impact of short video platforms on online marketing and advertising is undeniable. As these platforms continue to grow in popularity and evolve, businesses that are able to effectively leverage them will be well-positioned to reach and engage with their target audience in new and exciting ways.

Vlogging and short video platforms have become powerful tools for businesses to connect with their audiences and promote their products or services. Here are some of the benefits:

1. Increased reach and engagement: Vlogging and short video platforms have enormous potential for reach and engagement. Vloggers and short video creators can build massive followings and generate high levels of engagement through their content. This can translate into increased visibility and brand awareness for businesses that collaborate with them.

2. Authenticity: Vlogging and short video platforms allow businesses to showcase their products or services in an authentic and relatable way. Vloggers and short video creators often have a personal connection with their audiences, which can help businesses build trust and credibility.
3. Cost-effectiveness: Compared to traditional advertising channels, vlogging and short video platforms are relatively cost-effective. Businesses can collaborate with creators to produce content that promotes their brand without breaking the bank.
4. Flexibility: Vlogging and short video platforms allow businesses to be flexible with their marketing strategies. They can produce a wide range of content, from product reviews to tutorials, and adapt their content to changing trends and market demands.
5. Virality: Vlogging and short video platforms have the potential to go viral, meaning that a video or content can be shared rapidly and widely, leading to exponential exposure and brand awareness for the business.

In short, vlogging and short video platforms offer businesses an opportunity to reach a wider audience, generate authentic engagement, and promote their products or services in a cost-effective way. By collaborating with popular creators, businesses can tap into the power of these platforms and leverage their benefits for increased visibility and growth.

One of the main benefits of vlogging and short video platforms for businesses is the increased engagement with younger audiences. As younger generations become more reliant on digital media for entertainment and information, businesses must adapt their marketing strategies to effectively reach them.

Vlogging and short video platforms have emerged as powerful tools for businesses to connect with younger audiences. These platforms offer a unique opportunity for brands to showcase their products and services in a way that is engaging, entertaining, and relatable to younger consumers.

One of the reasons these platforms are so effective is their ability to quickly capture the attention of viewers. With short attention spans becoming increasingly common among younger audiences, the short, snappy format of vlogs and short videos is perfect for grabbing and holding their attention. This means that businesses have a greater chance of capturing the interest of younger consumers and making an impression on them.

Additionally, vlogging and short video platforms offer businesses the opportunity to showcase their brand personality in a more informal and relatable way. This is particularly important for younger consumers who value authenticity and transparency in the brands they support. By sharing behind-the-scenes footage, product demos, and candid moments, businesses can build a deeper connection with their audience and create a sense of community around their brand.

Another benefit of vlogging and short video platforms for businesses is their ability to generate user-generated content. User-generated content, or UGC, is any content created by consumers that features a brand or its products. This can include things like customer reviews, social media posts, and vlogs. UGC is particularly effective for building brand awareness and trust among younger audiences, who are more likely to trust the opinions of their peers than traditional advertising.

By encouraging users to create and share their own content featuring their products, businesses can tap into the power of UGC and build a community of loyal brand advocates. This can lead to increased brand awareness, more social media engagement, and ultimately, increased sales.

Improved brand awareness and visibility are two significant benefits of vlogging and short video platforms for businesses. These platforms offer a unique opportunity for businesses to showcase their products or services to a wider audience in an engaging and creative way.

One of the main advantages of vlogging and short video platforms is their ability to reach younger audiences. According to recent studies, the majority of social media users are between the ages of 18-29, with video platforms being particularly popular among this demographic. By creating content for these platforms, businesses have the opportunity to engage with a younger audience that may not be as responsive to traditional forms of advertising.

Moreover, vlogging and short video platforms offer businesses the opportunity to increase their brand awareness and visibility. These platforms have millions of active users who are constantly consuming content, and businesses can leverage this by creating content that is engaging, informative, and entertaining. By doing so, businesses can effectively introduce their brand to a wider audience and create a lasting impression.

Short videos also have the added benefit of being highly shareable. With the click of a button, users can share videos with their friends and followers, leading to an even wider reach for businesses. This can result in increased organic traffic to a business's website or social media profiles, leading to a boost in brand visibility and potentially even increased sales.

Another advantage of vlogging and short video platforms is their ability to create a more personal connection between businesses and their audience. By featuring real people, behind-the-scenes footage, and candid moments, businesses can humanize their brand and connect with their audience on a deeper level. This can lead to increased trust and loyalty from consumers, as they feel like they are interacting with a real person rather than a faceless corporation.

Overall, the benefits of vlogging and short video platforms for businesses are clear. These platforms offer a unique opportunity to reach a younger audience, increase brand awareness and visibility, and create a more personal connection with consumers. By leveraging these platforms effectively, businesses can enhance their online presence and potentially even drive sales.

The emergence of vlogging and short video platforms has created new opportunities for businesses to reach their target audience and promote their brand. One of the key benefits of using these platforms is the increased potential for viral content and word-of-mouth marketing.

Viral content refers to content that spreads rapidly and widely across the internet, often through social media platforms, and can generate significant attention and buzz for the creator. Vlogging and short video platforms provide a unique opportunity for businesses to create and share content that has the potential to go viral and reach a massive audience.

One of the most well-known examples of viral content on a short video platform is the "Renegade" dance. The dance, created by 14-year-old Jalaiah Harmon, quickly gained popularity on the platform and was performed by celebrities and influencers alike. The trend helped to bring attention to Harmon's talent and helped her to gain a following on the platform.

Viral content has the potential to generate significant brand awareness and engagement for businesses. It can also lead to increased sales and revenue, as consumers are more likely to purchase products or services from a brand that has gained their attention and interest.

In addition to viral content, vlogging and short video platforms also provide opportunities for word-of-mouth marketing. Word-of-mouth marketing refers to the practice of promoting a product or service through personal recommendations from satisfied customers. Vlogging and short video platforms provide a unique opportunity for businesses to engage with their audience and encourage them to share their experiences with others.

One example of successful word-of-mouth marketing on a short video platform is the "haul" trend. In a haul video, a vlogger shares their recent purchases from a specific brand or store, often providing reviews and recommendations to their audience. This type of content can be highly influential, as viewers are more likely to trust the opinion of someone they follow and admire.

By leveraging the power of viral content and word-of-mouth marketing, businesses can greatly increase their visibility and reach on vlogging and short video platforms. However, it is important to approach these strategies with caution and authenticity. Consumers can quickly detect disingenuous or forced marketing tactics, which can lead to negative backlash and damage to the brand's reputation.

In summary, the potential for viral content and word-of-mouth marketing on vlogging and short video platforms is a major benefit for businesses. By creating engaging and authentic content, brands can greatly increase their visibility and reach on these platforms, leading to increased brand awareness and potential for sales.

Challenges:

The emergence of vlogging and short video platforms has revolutionized the way businesses approach online marketing and advertising. However, along with the benefits, there are also challenges that businesses must navigate when utilizing these platforms. In this section, we will explore some of the common challenges businesses face when using vlogging and short video platforms, and provide practical advice for overcoming these challenges to effectively leverage these powerful tools.

One of the biggest challenges businesses face when using vlogging and short video platforms is maintaining authenticity and genuineness in sponsored content. As these platforms continue to grow in popularity, many businesses have turned to influencers and vloggers to promote their products and services.

While these collaborations can be effective in reaching a wider audience and boosting sales, it is important for businesses to approach them with caution. If not executed properly, sponsored content can come across as inauthentic and disingenuous, ultimately damaging the reputation of both the business and the influencer.

Consumers today value authenticity and transparency more than ever before. They are quick to detect when content is overly promotional or lacks sincerity. This can lead to a loss of trust in the influencer and the brand they are promoting.

To stay authentic and genuine in sponsored content, businesses should prioritize finding influencers and vloggers who align with their brand values and messaging. It is important for businesses to work with influencers who genuinely believe in their products or services and are passionate about promoting them.

Additionally, businesses should encourage influencers to be transparent about sponsored content and disclose their partnerships with the brand. This not only builds trust with the audience, but also ensures compliance with advertising regulations and guidelines.

It is also important for businesses to give influencers creative freedom and not impose too many restrictions on the content they create. This allows for a more authentic and natural approach to promoting the brand, rather than a forced and scripted one.

In the world of vlogging and short video platforms, content is king. With the rise of short video platforms, businesses are finding it increasingly important to keep up with the fast pace of content creation in order to stay relevant and engaged with their audiences.

One of the biggest challenges that businesses face when it comes to creating content for these platforms is the need to produce content quickly and consistently. With the short-form nature of these platforms, businesses need to create a high volume of content in order to keep their audiences engaged.

This can be particularly challenging for businesses that are new to the world of vlogging and short video platforms, as they may not have the resources or experience to produce content at the required speed and quality. It can also be challenging for businesses that are used to producing longer-form content, as they need to adapt their content creation processes to fit the shorter format.

For example, a business that is used to creating long-form videos may struggle to adapt their content to fit the short-form format. They may need to completely re-think their content strategy and come up with new ideas that can be communicated in a shorter amount of time.

Another challenge that businesses face when it comes to creating content for vlogging and short video platforms is the need to stay current and relevant. With the fast pace of content creation on these platforms, it can be easy for businesses to fall behind and become less visible to their audiences.

This is particularly true on platforms for short videos, where trends and challenges can emerge and disappear within a matter of days. In order to stay relevant and engaged with their audiences, businesses need to be able to quickly identify and adapt to these trends and challenges, while also maintaining their own unique brand voice and identity.

For example, a business that wants to create content around a popular trend may need to quickly come up with a creative and unique twist that still aligns with their brand values and messaging.

Overall, keeping up with the fast pace of content creation on vlogging and short video platforms can be a significant challenge for businesses. However, by staying creative, adaptable, and committed to delivering high-quality content, businesses can successfully navigate these challenges and use these platforms to reach and engage with their audiences in new and exciting ways.

Standing out in a saturated market is one of the major challenges businesses face when it comes to vlogging and short video platforms. With so many creators and businesses using these platforms, it can be difficult to make a name for oneself and capture the attention of the audience.

One effective strategy for standing out is to create content that is unique and visually appealing. This can be achieved through the use of creative and eye-catching visuals, as well as by offering fresh and innovative ideas. It is also important to have a consistent brand identity and message that resonates with the target audience.

Another strategy is to collaborate with other creators or brands in order to expand one's reach and tap into new audiences. By working with other businesses or influencers, it is possible to gain exposure to their followers and reach a wider audience.

However, it is important to ensure that collaborations are genuine and align with one's brand values and message. Partnering with other creators or brands solely for the purpose of gaining more followers or exposure can come across as inauthentic and may not resonate with the audience.

Another challenge in standing out in a saturated market is the need to constantly adapt and evolve. As trends and consumer preferences change, businesses must be able to keep up and offer fresh and innovative content that meets the needs and interests of the audience.

This requires a willingness to experiment and take risks, as well as a commitment to ongoing learning and development. It is also important to stay up-to-date with industry trends and best practices, and to seek out new tools and technologies that can help enhance content creation and delivery.

Standing out in a saturated market requires a combination of creativity, authenticity, collaboration, adaptability, and ongoing learning and development. By staying true to one's brand values and message, while also embracing new ideas and approaches, businesses can carve out a unique and successful niche in the world of vlogging and short video platforms.

Best Practices for Vlogging and Short Video Platforms

Businesses must stay on top of the latest trends and technologies to remain relevant and competitive. Vlogging and short video platforms have become increasingly popular in recent years, offering businesses a unique opportunity to reach and engage with audiences in new and exciting ways. However, with the benefits come challenges, and it is essential for businesses to understand the best practices for utilizing these platforms effectively.

In this section, we will explore the best practices for vlogging and short video platforms, including tips for creating engaging content, building a strong following, and utilizing these platforms to achieve your marketing goals. From developing a content strategy to optimizing your videos for maximum reach and engagement, these best practices will help businesses navigate the rapidly evolving landscape of vlogging and short video platforms.

Developing a unique and authentic brand is essential for businesses that want to succeed on vlogging and short video platforms. With so many users and content creators on these platforms, standing out from the crowd can be a difficult task. However, a strong brand can help businesses differentiate themselves and build a loyal following.

The first step in developing a strong brand is to understand your target audience. Who are they, what are their interests, and what kind of content do they enjoy? Use this information to create content that resonates with your audience and speaks to their interests.

Another important aspect of developing a strong brand is consistency. Consistency in your content, style, and messaging helps to establish a recognizable and memorable brand identity. This means using consistent visual elements such as color schemes, fonts, and logos, as well as consistent messaging and tone in your videos.

It's also important to be authentic and genuine in your content. Consumers can quickly sniff out inauthenticity and will be turned off by overly-promotional or insincere content. Instead, focus on creating content that is informative, entertaining, and adds value for your audience.

Collaborations and partnerships with other creators can also be a powerful way to build your brand and reach a wider audience. Collaborating with other creators in your industry or niche can help you tap into their existing audience and gain exposure to new viewers.

it's important to stay up to date on the latest trends and best practices in vlogging and short video platforms. This means staying active on the platform, engaging with your audience, and continuously experimenting and refining your content strategy.

In the world of vlogging and short video platforms, creating engaging and visually appealing content is crucial for standing out in a crowded market. With the rise of platforms, businesses and influencers alike are competing for attention in a fast-paced environment where users can quickly scroll past content that doesn't catch their eye.

To create engaging content, it's important to consider the platform and its unique features. For example, some platforms are known for its use of music and the ability to add text overlays and special effects, while Reels allows users to add filters and AR effects. Utilizing these features can help make content more visually appealing and shareable.

Additionally, it's important to consider the target audience and their interests. For example, a fashion brand targeting a younger demographic may create content featuring trendy outfits and makeup tutorials, while a fitness brand may create workout videos or healthy recipe demonstrations.

Collaborating with other vloggers or influencers can also be a great way to create engaging content and expand reach. By partnering with someone with a similar target audience and aesthetic, businesses can create content that is both authentic and appealing.

When it comes to visuals, it's important to prioritize high-quality images and videos. Investing in equipment such as a high-quality camera and lighting can make a significant difference in the overall quality of content. Additionally, utilizing editing tools and software can help enhance visuals and create a cohesive brand aesthetic.

Businesses should prioritize creating content that is both entertaining and informative. Whether it's providing tips and tricks related to a specific industry or showcasing behind-the-scenes footage, content that provides value to viewers is more likely to keep them engaged and coming back for more.

Collaborating with other creators and brands is a powerful way to increase visibility and expand reach on vlogging and short video platforms. By teaming up with other creators or partnering with brands, vloggers and short video creators can create unique and engaging content that appeals to a wider audience.

One popular form of collaboration is the "collab video," where two or more creators come together to create a video. Collab videos can take many forms, such as challenges, Q&A sessions, or simply sharing tips and advice. These videos allow creators to showcase their personalities and unique perspectives, while also introducing their audience to a new creator and potentially gaining new followers.

Partnering with brands is another way for vloggers and short video creators to expand their reach and monetize their content. Brands may reach out to creators directly or through influencer marketing platforms to collaborate on sponsored content. These collaborations can take many forms, such as sponsored posts or product reviews, and can be a lucrative source of income for creators.

However, it's important for creators to carefully consider the brands they choose to partner with and ensure that the partnership aligns with their values and content. Collaborating with a brand that doesn't align with their values or audience could damage their reputation and credibility.

Another form of collaboration is joining or creating a creator network or community. These communities allow creators to connect with other like-minded individuals and collaborate on projects or share tips and advice. They also provide a support system for creators, as creating content can be a solitary activity.

In addition to collaborations, it's important for vloggers and short video creators to consistently create high-quality content that is visually appealing and engaging. This requires investing in quality equipment, such as cameras and lighting, and editing software to create a polished final product.

Creators should prioritize building a strong and engaged community by responding to comments and messages, and engaging with their audience through polls and Q&A sessions. By fostering a strong relationship with their audience, creators can create a loyal following that will continue to support them and their content.

Collaborating with other creators and brands can be a powerful way for vloggers and short video creators to expand their reach and monetize their content. By creating engaging and visually appealing content, joining creator communities, and building a strong relationship with their audience, creators can stand out in a crowded market and build a successful career on vlogging and short video platforms.

Future Trends and Innovations in Vlogging and Short Video Platforms

As the online world continues to evolve and new technologies emerge, vlogging and short video platforms have become an increasingly popular way for businesses and individuals to connect with their audiences. In this section, we will explore some of the emerging trends and innovations in the world of vlogging and short video platforms, and how they may shape the future of online marketing and advertising.

From new features and tools on existing platforms to the rise of new platforms, the landscape of vlogging and short video content is constantly changing. By staying up-to-date with these trends and innovations, businesses and individuals can stay ahead of the curve and effectively reach and engage with their target audience. Let's take a closer look at what the future may hold for vlogging and short video platforms.

As technology continues to advance, vlogging and short video platforms are beginning to integrate e-commerce and shopping features into their platforms. This integration provides businesses with a new way to sell products and services directly to their audience, while also providing consumers with a seamless shopping experience.

One example of this integration is shopping feature. These platforms allow businesses to tag products in their posts, which leads to a product page where users can purchase the item directly from the app. This feature allows businesses to reach their audience in a more direct and engaging way, and also allows consumers to easily shop for the products they see on their feed.

One of the most popular short video platform is also exploring e-commerce integration, with the launch of their "Shopping" feature. This feature allows brands to link their product catalog to their account, and users can purchase products without leaving the app.

The integration of e-commerce and shopping features in vlogging and short video platforms is a trend that is expected to continue to grow. As these platforms continue to expand and become more advanced, businesses will have even more opportunities to reach their target audience and drive sales through these channels.

However, as with any new technology, there are potential drawbacks and concerns with this integration. For example, there may be questions around data privacy and security, as well as potential issues with the authenticity of sponsored content that is linked to shopping features. It will be important for businesses to navigate these potential challenges and ensure that they are delivering an ethical and transparent shopping experience for their customers.

The use of augmented and virtual reality (AR/VR) is another emerging trend in vlogging and short video platforms. AR/VR technology has the potential to revolutionize the way businesses create and share content, as it allows for immersive and interactive experiences for viewers.

One example of the use of AR/VR in short video platforms is Lens Studio, which allows users to create their own AR filters and effects for their videos. Brands have used this feature to create engaging and interactive experiences for their audiences, such as allowing them to try on virtual makeup or accessories.

Another example is the use of virtual reality in travel vlogs, where viewers can experience a 360-degree view of a destination and feel like they are actually there. This creates a more immersive and engaging experience for the viewer, and can potentially lead to increased interest and sales in travel-related products and services.

As AR/VR technology continues to advance and become more accessible, it is likely that we will see more businesses incorporating it into their vlogging and short video content. This will require brands to invest in the necessary technology and resources to create high-quality AR/VR experiences, but the potential benefits in terms of engagement and conversion rates make it a worthwhile investment.

The popularity of short-form video content shows no signs of slowing down. With the rise of short video platforms, businesses and creators are increasingly turning to these bite-sized videos to engage with their audiences.

One of the main advantages of short-form video is its ability to capture and hold the viewer's attention. With shorter attention spans and an abundance of content competing for viewers' time, it's important to make an impact quickly. Short-form videos that are visually engaging and easy to consume are more likely to be watched to completion and shared with others.

Short-form videos also offer a greater potential for virality, as they are more likely to be shared on social media and reach a wider audience. This can lead to increased brand awareness and the potential for new customers.

In addition, short-form videos are typically easier and quicker to produce than longer-form content like vlogs. This can be a significant advantage for businesses with limited resources or those looking to produce content at a faster pace.

However, creating effective short-form videos requires a different approach than longer-form content. It's important to focus on visual storytelling and capturing attention quickly, while still conveying a clear message and staying true to the brand's voice and values.

Overall, the continued rise of short-form video content presents both opportunities and challenges for businesses and creators. By understanding the unique advantages of this format and developing a strategy tailored to their audience and goals, businesses can leverage short-form videos to effectively engage with their audience and stay relevant in a constantly evolving digital landscape.

Vlogging and short video platforms have become an integral part of the online marketplace, providing businesses with new opportunities to engage with younger audiences, increase brand awareness, and tap into the potential of viral content. However, businesses must also navigate the challenges of staying authentic in sponsored content, keeping up with the fast pace of content creation, and standing out in a saturated market.

To succeed on these platforms, businesses must focus on developing a unique and authentic brand, creating visually appealing and engaging content, and collaborating with other creators and brands. Furthermore, future trends and innovations in the industry, such as the integration of e-commerce and shopping features, the use of augmented and virtual reality, and the continued rise of short-form video content, provide exciting opportunities for businesses to continue growing their presence and connecting with their audiences.

As businesses adapt to the evolving landscape of vlogging and short video platforms, they can leverage the power of these platforms to build stronger relationships with their customers, increase their reach, and ultimately drive growth and success in the online marketplace.

Freelance Marketplaces

Freelance marketplaces have become a popular and accessible way for businesses and individuals to connect with a vast network of skilled professionals who can provide the necessary services remotely. The freelance economy has been growing rapidly in recent years, with more people turning to freelancing as a full-time career or as a way to supplement their income. This has led to the rise of online freelance marketplaces, which have transformed the way businesses and freelancers interact and collaborate.

The freelance marketplace model has several benefits for both businesses and freelancers. For businesses, it provides access to a diverse pool of talent from around the world, allowing them to find the right person for the job quickly and easily. Freelancers also benefit from increased access to job opportunities, as well as the ability to work from anywhere in the world and have more control over their schedule.

One of the key advantages of freelance marketplaces is the flexibility they offer. Businesses can hire freelancers on a project-by-project basis, allowing them to scale up or down as needed. This allows businesses to save money by avoiding the cost of hiring full-time staff, while also benefiting from the expertise of specialized professionals. Freelancers, in turn, can choose which projects to work on and set their own rates, giving them greater control over their workload and income.

Another benefit of freelance marketplaces is the ability to work with professionals from around the world. This allows businesses to tap into a global talent pool and find experts in their field, regardless of their location. Freelancers can also benefit from the ability to work with clients from different parts of the world, gaining exposure to new cultures and ideas.

However, there are also challenges that come with using freelance marketplaces. One of the biggest challenges is finding the right freelancer for the job. With so many freelancers to choose from, businesses can struggle to identify the most qualified candidate. Freelancers may also face challenges in standing out from the competition and winning new business. Additionally, both businesses and freelancers may face issues with payment and contract disputes.

Despite these challenges, the freelance marketplace model has proven to be a popular and effective way for businesses and freelancers to connect and collaborate. In the following sections, we will explore the benefits and challenges of using freelance marketplaces, as well as best practices for businesses and freelancers to succeed in this rapidly growing industry.

The rise of the gig economy has led to an increase in the number of freelance professionals in various fields, ranging from graphic designers to content writers to software developers. With the growing demand for flexible work arrangements and the ability to work remotely, freelance marketplaces have become an integral part of the online marketplace ecosystem. These marketplaces connect freelancers with clients looking for specific services, and they offer a wide range of benefits for both parties. However, there are also some challenges that come with using these platforms.

Advantages of Freelance Marketplaces

1. Access to a Global Talent Pool
   Freelance marketplaces provide businesses with access to a global pool of talent. These marketplaces have freelancers from

all over the world, allowing businesses to find professionals with the skills they need, regardless of their location. This means businesses can find the best talent for their projects without being limited by geography.For freelancers, these marketplaces provide access to clients from all over the world, increasing their earning potential and allowing them to work with a diverse range of clients.

2. Cost Savings

   Using freelance marketplaces can be more cost-effective for businesses compared to hiring full-time employees. Freelancers charge on a per-project or hourly basis, which means businesses only pay for the work they need, without having to provide additional benefits and perks that come with full-time employment.

   For freelancers, these marketplaces provide an opportunity to earn a higher hourly rate compared to traditional employment. Additionally, freelancers can save on the costs associated with working in a traditional office, such as commuting expenses and work attire.

3. Flexibility

   Freelance marketplaces provide flexibility for both businesses and freelancers. Businesses can hire freelancers on a project-by-project basis, allowing them to scale up or down as needed. Freelancers, on the other hand, have the flexibility to choose the projects they want to work on and the hours they want to work.

4. Speed and Efficiency

   Freelance marketplaces provide businesses with access to a large pool of pre-vetted professionals, making the hiring process faster and more efficient. Businesses can quickly find and hire freelancers for their projects without having to spend time and resources on recruitment.

Challenges of Freelance Marketplaces

1. Quality Control

   One of the biggest challenges of using freelance marketplaces is ensuring the quality of work delivered by the freelancers. While these marketplaces have review systems in place, there is no guarantee that the work will meet the expectations of the client.

2. Communication and Time Zone Differences

   Freelance marketplaces can have freelancers from all over the world, which can lead to communication challenges due to time zone differences and language barriers. This can result in delays and miscommunications, which can impact project timelines and deliverables.

3. Legal and Contractual Issues

   Using freelance marketplaces can also create legal and contractual issues for businesses. It can be difficult to ensure that the freelancers are legally authorized to work in the country where the work is being done, and there may be issues with ownership of intellectual property and confidentiality.

   For freelancers, there can be challenges in ensuring they are paid on time and that their work is protected by a legally binding contract.

4. Competition

   Freelance marketplaces are highly competitive, with freelancers from all over the world vying for the same projects. This means that freelancers must constantly update their skills and pricing strategies to remain competitive and attract clients.

Freelance marketplaces have grown rapidly in recent years and have become an integral part of the global economy. These platforms offer a range of benefits for businesses and freelancers, but they also come with drawbacks that need to be considered. In this section, we will explore the benefits and drawbacks of freelance marketplaces in detail.

Benefits of Freelance Marketplaces

1. Access to a large pool of talent: Freelance marketplaces provide businesses with access to a vast pool of talent from around the world. This allows businesses to find the right talent for their specific needs, regardless of location or time zone.
   For freelancers, this means having access to a global customer base, which can help to increase their earning potential and expand their network.
2. Cost-effective: Freelance marketplaces are often more cost-effective for businesses compared to traditional hiring methods. This is because businesses can hire freelancers on a project-by-project basis, rather than committing to a full-time employee.
   For freelancers, freelance marketplaces offer a way to earn a living without the overhead costs associated with starting a business or working in a traditional office setting.
3. Flexibility: Freelance marketplaces offer both businesses and freelancers a high degree of flexibility. For businesses, this means being able to scale their workforce up or down as needed, without the need for long-term commitments. For freelancers, this means having the ability to work on their own terms, choose their own clients, and set their own schedules.
4. Faster turnaround times: With freelance marketplaces, businesses can find the right talent quickly and easily, often with just a few clicks of a button. This can result in faster turnaround times for projects and a quicker time-to-market.

Drawbacks of Freelance Marketplaces

1. Limited control: Freelance marketplaces often offer limited control over the work being performed, as businesses are not directly managing the freelancer. This can lead to communication breakdowns, missed deadlines, and lower quality work.
   For freelancers, limited control can also mean that they may be subjected to unreasonable client demands or expectations.

2. High competition: Freelance marketplaces are highly competitive, with thousands of freelancers competing for the same projects. This can make it challenging for freelancers to stand out and for businesses to find the right talent.
3. Limited support: Freelance marketplaces often offer limited support to both businesses and freelancers. This can include limited customer support, lack of dispute resolution processes, and limited access to legal resources.
4. Security concerns: Freelance marketplaces may be susceptible to security breaches, such as identity theft, hacking, or fraud. This can put both businesses and freelancers at risk and can result in financial losses.

Despite these drawbacks, freelance marketplaces remain a popular choice for businesses and freelancers alike. In the next section, we will explore the different types of freelance marketplaces and how they operate.

Freelance marketplaces have been growing rapidly in recent years, providing businesses with a flexible and cost-effective way to hire skilled professionals for various projects. However, like any other business decision, using freelance marketplaces comes with both advantages and disadvantages. In this section, we will analyze the pros and cons of using freelance marketplaces.

Pros:

1. Access to a global talent pool: Freelance marketplaces provide businesses with access to a vast network of skilled professionals from all around the world. This allows businesses to find the best talent for their projects, regardless of location.
2. Cost-effective: Hiring freelancers through marketplaces can be more cost-effective than hiring full-time employees. Freelancers are often paid on a project-by-project basis, which can save businesses money on salaries, benefits, and other overhead costs.

3. Flexibility: Freelance marketplaces offer businesses the flexibility to hire professionals on a short-term or project basis, allowing them to scale their workforce up or down as needed.
4. Expertise: Freelancers on these platforms often have niche areas of expertise, making it easier for businesses to find professionals with the specific skills they need for their projects.
5. Time-saving: Hiring freelancers through marketplaces can save businesses time on the recruitment process, as these platforms provide access to a large pool of pre-vetted professionals.

Cons:

1. Quality control: One of the biggest challenges of using freelance marketplaces is ensuring the quality of work delivered by freelancers. It can be difficult to assess the skills and experience of freelancers, and there is always a risk of receiving subpar work.
2. Communication issues: Freelancers on these platforms may be located in different time zones or have language barriers, making communication challenging and potentially slowing down project timelines.
3. Dependability: Freelancers on these platforms may have multiple projects going on at the same time, which can lead to delays and missed deadlines.
4. Lack of loyalty: Since freelancers are not full-time employees, they may not have the same level of commitment and loyalty to the business as regular employees.
5. Legal issues: Freelancers may not have the same legal protections as full-time employees, which can create legal and financial risks for businesses.

Examples:

1. Access to a global talent pool: A small business in the US may need a website designer with specific skills, but may not be able to find the right person locally. By using a freelance

marketplace, they can find a website designer from another country who has the skills they need.

2. Cost-effective: A marketing agency may need a writer for a specific project, but hiring a full-time writer may not be cost-effective. By using a freelance marketplace, they can hire a writer on a project basis and save money on salaries and benefits.

3. Quality control: A business may hire a freelancer through a marketplace for a design project, but the freelancer may not deliver the quality of work expected. This can result in additional costs and delays for the business.

4. Communication issues: A business may hire a freelancer from a different time zone, which can lead to communication issues and slow down project timelines.

5. Legal issues: A business may inadvertently misclassify a freelancer as an independent contractor instead of an employee, which can result in legal and financial risks.

Best Practices for Freelancers on Freelance Marketplaces:

The freelance marketplace has become a highly competitive space, with millions of freelancers from all over the world offering their skills and services to potential clients. In order to stand out from the crowd and succeed as a freelancer, it is essential to adopt certain best practices that will help you build a strong reputation and win clients. In this section, we will discuss some of the best practices for freelancers on freelance marketplaces.

1. Build a strong profile:
   Your profile is your first impression on potential clients, and it needs to be strong and compelling. Make sure your profile is complete and showcases your skills, experience, and expertise. Use a professional profile picture, and write a clear and concise summary of your skills and services. Make sure to highlight your unique selling proposition and what sets you apart from other freelancers.

2. Be selective with projects:

It can be tempting to apply for every project that comes your way, but it is important to be selective and only apply for projects that align with your skills and interests. This will not only help you deliver high-quality work, but it will also help you build a portfolio of work that showcases your strengths and areas of expertise.

3. Communicate clearly and professionally:
   Clear and professional communication is essential for building trust with clients. Make sure to respond to messages promptly and keep clients updated on your progress. Ask questions when you are unclear about a project, and be open to feedback and constructive criticism.

4. Deliver high-quality work:
   Your work is a reflection of your skills and reputation, so it is essential to deliver high-quality work that meets or exceeds your client's expectations. Make sure to meet deadlines and pay attention to details, and always strive to deliver work that you are proud of.

5. Build long-term relationships:
   Building long-term relationships with clients is essential for ongoing success as a freelancer. Make sure to follow up with clients after a project is completed and stay in touch. Keep them updated on your availability and offer suggestions for future projects that may be of interest to them.

6. Stay up-to-date on industry trends:
   The freelance marketplace is constantly evolving, so it is important to stay up-to-date on industry trends and best practices. Attend industry events and webinars, read industry blogs and publications, and network with other freelancers to stay informed and competitive.

7. Be flexible and adaptable:
   The freelance marketplace can be unpredictable, so it is important to be flexible and adaptable. Be open to new opportunities and challenges, and be willing to adjust your rates or approach to meet the needs of a particular project or client.

Trends and Innovations in Freelance Marketplaces:

As the world of work continues to evolve, so do the freelance marketplaces that connect independent contractors with businesses seeking their services. These marketplaces have seen significant growth in recent years, and they show no signs of slowing down. In this section, we will explore the latest trends and innovations in the freelance marketplace industry.

1. Niche Marketplaces
    As the freelance marketplace industry continues to grow, more and more niche marketplaces are emerging. These marketplaces are designed to connect businesses with freelancers who have specialized skills in a particular industry or niche. For example, there are marketplaces specifically for writers, designers, developers, and even lawyers. One example of a niche marketplace is a platform, which specializes in connecting businesses with top-tier freelance developers and designers. It's rigorous screening process ensures that only the top 3% of applicants are accepted, making it an attractive option for businesses looking for high-quality talent.
    Another example is Writer Access, which specializes in connecting businesses with freelance writers who have expertise in a particular industry or topic. Writer Access uses a proprietary algorithm to match businesses with writers who have the right skills and experience for their specific needs.

2. Collaboration and Project Management Tools
    As more businesses turn to freelance marketplaces to find talent, the need for effective collaboration and project management tools has become increasingly important. Many freelance marketplaces now offer built-in project management tools to help businesses and freelancers work together more effectively.
    For example, one of the largest freelance marketplaces, offers a suite of project management tools that allow businesses to manage their projects, communicate with freelancers, and track

their progress all in one place. These tools include time tracking, invoicing, and file sharing capabilities.

Similarly, another platform offers a project management tool called Milestones, which allows businesses to break their projects into smaller, manageable pieces and track their progress in real-time. Milestones also includes a messaging system that allows businesses and freelancers to communicate with each other throughout the project.

3. AI Matching and Screening

    Another trend in the freelance marketplace industry is the use of artificial intelligence (AI) to match businesses with the right freelancers for their projects. AI can help streamline the hiring process by automatically screening applicants and matching them with the most appropriate projects.

    For example, a platform uses AI to screen applicants based on their skills, experience, and other factors. The platform's AI algorithm analyzes data from applicants' profiles, work history, and skill tests to determine if they are a good fit for the platform.

    Similarly, another marketplace uses an AI-powered matching system to match businesses with the most suitable freelancers for their projects. The system analyzes factors such as the freelancer's skills, experience, and portfolio to make a match.

4. Blockchain Technology

    Blockchain technology, which is best known for powering cryptocurrencies such as Bitcoin, has also found its way into the freelance marketplace industry. Blockchain technology can be used to create decentralized marketplaces that eliminate the need for intermediaries and increase transparency and security. One example is a blockchain-based freelance marketplace, which allows freelancers to create their own profiles and list their services for hire. Clients can then search for and hire freelancers directly through the platform, using a cryptocurrency.

    Another example is a blockchain-based platform that connects businesses with freelancers. The platform uses smart contracts to ensure that payments are made automatically and securely, without the need for intermediaries.

The freelance marketplace industry continues to grow and evolve, driven by the changing needs of businesses and the increasing number of people choosing to work as freelancers. The trends and innovations discussed in this section are just a few examples of the many changes taking place in this industry.

Generating Revenue from Reels

One of the newest features introduced is Reels, a short-form video format that allows users to create and share 15-second videos with their followers and on the Reels Explore page.

Reels provides a unique opportunity for individuals and businesses alike to generate revenue by creating engaging content that resonates with their target audience. In fact, Reels has become a popular tool for influencers and brands to promote their products and services, as well as for creators to showcase their talents and build their personal brands.

In this chapter, we will explore the various ways in which individuals and businesses can leverage Reels to generate revenue. We will examine the key benefits of Reels as a marketing tool, the challenges of creating successful Reels content, and the best practices for using Reels to drive revenue growth.

Whether you are an influencer looking to monetize your social media presence or a business seeking to expand your online marketing strategy, Reels offers a powerful platform for reaching and engaging with your target audience. By following the strategies and tips outlined in this chapter, you can tap into the full potential of Reels and build a strong and profitable presence on the platform.

The Basics of Reels:

In recent years, This platform has become a crucial platform for businesses and influencers to market their brand and connect with their audience. With the rise of short-form video content, The platform launched a new feature called Reels in August 2020. This feature allows users to create and share 15-second videos set to music, with a variety of editing tools such as filters, effects, and text overlays.

Reels has quickly become a popular tool for businesses and influencers to engage with their audience, showcase their brand personality, and increase their reach on the platform. In this section, we will explore the basics of Reels, including how to create and share Reels, the different editing tools available, and the best practices for using Reels to promote your brand. Whether you're new to Reels or looking to improve your Reel strategy, this section will provide you with the essential knowledge and skills to succeed on the platform.

Creating and posting a Reel on is a straightforward process. Here are the steps to follow:

1. Open the app and swipe to the left to access the camera.
2. Select the "Reels" option from the bottom menu.
3. Choose the duration of your Reel. You can create a Reel that's up to 60 seconds long.
4. Use the camera to record your video. You can record multiple clips by pressing and holding the capture button. You can also use the timer and countdown features to help with your recording.
5. Edit your Reel. You can add music, text, filters, and other effects to your video.
6. Preview your Reel to make sure it looks how you want it to.
7. Write a caption and add hashtags to help people discover your Reel.
8. Choose where you want to post your Reel. You can post it to your Reels feed, your feed, or both.
9. Tap "Share" to post your Reel.

When creating a Reel, keep in mind that it's important to make it visually appealing and engaging. Use eye-catching visuals, interesting music, and creative effects to make your Reel stand out. Additionally, consider your target audience and what they would find interesting or useful. By creating Reels that resonate with your audience, you'll be more likely to attract new followers and grow your account.

To generate revenue from Reels, it's crucial to create content that resonates with your target audience and keeps them engaged. Here are some best practices for creating engaging Reels:

1. Keep it short and sweet: Reels are designed to be short-form videos, so keep your content concise and to the point. Aim for a length of 15-30 seconds to capture your audience's attention quickly and hold it throughout the video.
2. Be creative and unique: With so much content available on social media, it's important to stand out. Use your creativity to come up with unique ideas that haven't been done before. This could be anything from a funny skit to a unique dance move. Don't be afraid to experiment and try something new.
3. Use high-quality visuals and sound: Reels is a visual medium, so make sure your video is visually appealing. Use high-quality visuals and good lighting to make your video look professional. Additionally, make sure your audio is clear and easy to hear.
4. Incorporate trending topics: Stay up to date with the latest trends and incorporate them into your Reels. This could be a popular dance or a trending meme. By including trending topics, you can increase the visibility of your content and potentially attract new followers.
5. Include a call-to-action: At the end of your Reel, include a call-to-action (CTA) to encourage engagement from your audience. This could be anything from asking them to like and share your video to visiting your website or making a purchase.
6. Stay true to your brand: While it's important to be creative and unique, it's also important to stay true to your brand. Make sure your Reels align with your brand values and messaging. This will

help to build trust with your audience and establish a strong brand identity.

7. Post consistently: Consistency is key when it comes to social media. Aim to post Reels on a regular basis to keep your audience engaged and attract new followers. Posting consistently will also help you to establish a strong presence on the platform.

By following these best practices, you can create engaging and effective Reels that will help you to generate revenue on this platform.

Utilizing hashtags and captions for increased visibility:

Hashtags and captions are powerful tools for increasing the visibility of Reels and reaching a larger audience. Hashtags are a way of categorizing content and making it discoverable to users searching for a specific topic. When you add a hashtag to your Reel, it becomes part of that hashtag's feed, which means that anyone who searches for or follows that particular hashtag has the potential to see your content.

To use hashtags effectively, it's important to do some research and choose hashtags that are relevant to your content and have a significant following. You can use tools like Hashtagify or the explore page to find popular hashtags that are related to your niche. It's also a good idea to use a mix of broad and specific hashtags to reach both a large and targeted audience.

Captions are another important element of Reels that can help increase visibility and engagement. A caption provides context for your Reel and can encourage viewers to engage with your content by leaving comments, sharing or saving the Reel, or following your account. It's important to keep captions short and to the point, while also being descriptive and adding value to the content.

To create engaging captions, consider asking questions, providing additional information or context, or including a call-to-action. You can also use emojis to add personality and convey emotion. When writing captions, it's important to keep your audience in mind and use language that resonates with them.

In addition to using hashtags and captions, it's also important to engage with your audience by responding to comments and messages, and by participating in relevant conversations and communities on the platform. This can help build a loyal following and increase the visibility of your content over time.

Opportunities for Revenue Generation on Reels:

As Reels has gained popularity among users, it has also presented a new avenue for businesses and creators to generate revenue. With its short-form video format and high engagement rates, Reels has become an attractive platform for brands to reach their target audience and for creators to monetize their content. This section will explore the various opportunities for revenue generation on Reels, including sponsored content, affiliate marketing, and e-commerce integration. Additionally, we will discuss the benefits and challenges of each method and provide practical advice for businesses and creators looking to monetize their Reels content.

Sponsored content and brand partnership:

Sponsored content and brand partnerships have become an increasingly popular way for creators to generate revenue on Reels. These partnerships involve collaborations between creators and brands, where the creator creates content that promotes the brand's product or service.

Sponsored content can take many forms, such as product reviews, tutorials, or simply showcasing the brand's product in a creative way. The key is to ensure that the sponsored content aligns with the creator's brand and values, and that it is clearly disclosed as sponsored content to comply with advertising regulations.

One of the biggest benefits of sponsored content is the potential for a high payout. Brands are willing to pay top dollar to work with popular creators who have a large and engaged audience. However, it's important for creators to negotiate fair compensation and not undersell themselves in these partnerships.

Another benefit of sponsored content is that it can help to build credibility and trust with the creator's audience. If a creator promotes a product that they genuinely believe in and use themselves, their audience is more likely to trust their recommendation and potentially make a purchase.

However, it's important for creators to maintain authenticity and transparency in their sponsored content. Overly-promotional or inauthentic sponsored content can be a turn-off to audiences and lead to a loss of trust and credibility.

In addition to sponsored content, creators can also generate revenue through brand partnerships. This involves working with a brand on a longer-term basis, where the creator becomes an ambassador or representative for the brand. This can include creating sponsored content, attending events, or even developing their own product lines in collaboration with the brand.

Overall, sponsored content and brand partnerships can be a lucrative and mutually beneficial way for creators to generate revenue on Reels, but it's important to maintain authenticity and transparency in these collaborations to preserve the creator's credibility and trust with their audience.

Utilizing affiliate marketing::

In addition to sponsored content and brand partnerships, another way to generate revenue on Reels is through affiliate marketing. Affiliate marketing is a type of performance-based marketing in which an individual promotes a product and earns a commission for any resulting sales.

To utilize affiliate marketing on Reels, the first step is to find affiliate programs that align with your content and audience. This can involve researching and reaching out to companies in your niche or signing up for affiliate networks.

Once you have established affiliate partnerships, you can begin creating content that features products and includes affiliate links. It is important to disclose your affiliate relationship with your audience and to only promote products that you genuinely believe in and use yourself.

To maximize the effectiveness of your affiliate marketing efforts on Reels, it is important to create engaging and informative content that showcases the product in an authentic way. This can involve demonstrating the product in use, providing a review or comparison, or highlighting its features and benefits.

In addition to creating content, it can also be helpful to include calls to action encouraging your followers to use your affiliate link to purchase the product. This can involve including the link in your caption, adding it as a swipe-up link in your Story, or directing viewers to the link in the video itself.

Overall, affiliate marketing can be a valuable tool for generating revenue on Reels, particularly for creators with engaged and loyal audiences. By partnering with brands and promoting products that align with your content and audience, you can earn a commission while providing value to your followers.

In addition to sponsored content and affiliate marketing, Reels also offers monetization features that allow creators to earn revenue directly through the platform.

One such feature is IGTV ads, which allow creators to monetize their longer-form video content. To be eligible for IGTV ads, creators must have a "creator" or "business" account, be located in a supported country, and meet certain eligibility criteria, such as having a certain number of followers and engagement metrics. Once approved, creators can earn a portion of the revenue generated by ads that appear on their IGTV videos.

Another way to monetize through Reels is by utilizing shopping tags. With this feature, creators can tag products in their Reels, allowing viewers to easily purchase the products through in-app checkout feature. Creators can earn a commission on the sales generated through their shopping tags.

It's important to note that monetizing through features requires meeting certain eligibility criteria and following the platform's guidelines and policies. Additionally, creators should ensure that any sponsored or affiliate content is clearly disclosed to their audience to maintain transparency and credibility.

This platform has introduced several monetization options for creators, including the Creator Fund, which is an exclusive program that offers financial support to eligible creators. This program is still in the testing phase, but it has been rolled out in some countries, including the United States, the United Kingdom, and Canada.

To be eligible for the Creator Fund, creators must meet certain criteria, such as having a certain number of followers and meeting engagement metrics. If accepted, creators will receive a monthly payout based on their performance and engagement.

Another monetization option for creators is IGTV ads. The platform has introduced the option for creators to monetize their IGTV videos with ads, which are inserted during the video playback. Creators earn a share of the revenue generated by the ads, which is determined by the number of views and engagement on their videos.

It has also introduced shopping tags, which allow creators to tag products in their Reels and other content. When users click on the tag, they are directed to a product page where they can make a purchase. Creators earn a commission on sales generated through their tags.

Other monetization options for creators include sponsored posts, product placements, and collaborations with brands. Creators can also sell their own products or services, such as digital products, merchandise, or coaching services.

Overall, this platform has provided several options for creators to monetize their content on the platform, and as the platform continues to evolve, it is likely that more opportunities will arise for revenue generation.

Strategies for Building a Following and Increasing Engagement on Reels:

As the popularity of Reels continues to grow, so does the competition among creators vying for viewers' attention. Building a strong following and increasing engagement on Reels is crucial for monetizing the platform and generating revenue. In this section, we will discuss effective strategies for building a following and increasing engagement on Reels. From leveraging analytics to collaborating with other creators, these tips and tricks will help you stand out in a crowded marketplace and build a loyal audience.

Identifying and targeting a niche audience is an essential strategy for building a following and increasing engagement on Reels. When you create content that resonates with a specific group of people, you're more likely to attract a loyal following and drive engagement on your Reels.

The first step in identifying your niche audience is to understand your brand and the type of content you want to create. Once you have a clear idea of your brand identity and content focus, you can start to research your target audience. This includes analyzing the demographics, interests, and behavior of your potential followers.

One effective way to identify your niche audience is to use social media analytics tools. The platform provides insights into the demographics of your followers and the performance of your content. By analyzing this data, you can identify trends and patterns that can help you understand your audience better.

Another strategy is to engage with your audience directly through comments and direct messages. By building a relationship with your followers, you can learn more about their interests and preferences and tailor your content to their needs.

Once you've identified your niche audience, it's important to create content that resonates with them. This means using language, imagery, and topics that are relevant to your audience's interests and needs. You can also use hashtags and other tactics to make your content more discoverable to your target audience.

Finally, it's important to engage with your followers regularly to build a strong community around your brand. This means responding to comments and direct messages, asking for feedback, and creating a sense of shared identity with your followers. By building a strong relationship with your niche audience, you can drive engagement on your Reels and grow your following over time.

Consistent posting and engagement are crucial for building a following and increasing engagement on Reels. Just like any other social media platform, posting regularly and interacting with your audience is essential to keep them interested in your content and coming back for more.

When it comes to posting frequency, it's important to strike a balance between posting too often and not often enough. Posting too often can overwhelm your audience and lead to them unfollowing you, while not posting often enough can cause them to lose interest and forget about you. A good rule of thumb is to aim for at least three to four Reels per week, but don't be afraid to adjust based on your audience's preferences and engagement rates.

In addition to consistent posting, engaging with your followers is equally important. Responding to comments and direct messages can help foster a sense of community and make your followers feel valued. You can also ask for their input and feedback on your content, which can help you improve and create content that resonates with your audience.

Another way to increase engagement is by using the platform's interactive features, such as polls, quizzes, and questions. These features can encourage your followers to engage with your content and help you gain insights into their preferences and interests.

Finally, don't forget to leverage cross-promotion to drive traffic to your Reels. Share your Reels on other social media platforms, and consider collaborating with other users in your niche to reach a wider audience. By consistently posting and engaging with your audience, you can build a strong following on Reels and increase your chances of generating revenue.

Utilizing collaborations and cross-promotion with other creators can be an effective strategy for building a following and increasing engagement on Reels. Collaborating with other creators can help increase your reach and introduce you to new audiences who are interested in similar content.

One way to collaborate with other creators is through content collaborations. This involves creating a Reel with another creator, either in person or remotely, that showcases both of your talents and interests. This type of collaboration can help expose your content to a wider audience and can also help build relationships with other creators in your niche.

Another way to collaborate is through cross-promotion. This involves sharing each other's content and promoting each other's accounts on your respective platforms. For example, you can collaborate with a creator who has a larger following than you and ask them to share your Reels on their account, in exchange for you doing the same for them. This can help drive traffic to each other's pages and increase your overall reach and engagement.

It's important to note that when collaborating with other creators, it's crucial to choose someone who aligns with your brand values and content. Collaborating with someone who has vastly different content or values can harm your reputation and turn off your existing followers.

In addition to collaborating with other creators, you can also participate in challenges and trends. These can be a great way to increase your visibility and reach new audiences. By participating in popular challenges and trends, you can get your content in front of a larger audience who is already interested in that topic.

Overall, collaborations and cross-promotion with other creators, as well as participating in popular challenges and trends, can be effective strategies for building a following and increasing engagement on Reels. By working with others in your niche and participating in popular trends, you can increase your visibility and exposure to new audiences, ultimately leading to increased engagement and revenue opportunities.

Experimenting with new formats and trends is a crucial aspect of building a following and increasing engagement on Reels. As the platform continues to evolve, it is important for creators to stay up-to-date with the latest trends and adapt their content accordingly.

One trend that has gained popularity on Reels is the use of music and sound. Music is a key component of Reels, and incorporating popular songs and sounds into your content can help to increase engagement and reach. It is important to stay up-to-date with the latest music trends and to use high-quality sound in your videos.

Another trend that has emerged on Reels is the use of text overlays and visual effects. Adding text overlays to your videos can help to convey a message or add context to your content, while visual effects can make your videos more eye-catching and engaging. It is important to use these elements in a way that is tasteful and consistent with your brand image.

In addition to these trends, it is important to experiment with new formats and styles of content. For example, you may want to try creating tutorial-style videos, behind-the-scenes content, or even humorous skits. By testing new ideas and formats, you can gain valuable insights into what resonates with your audience and adjust your content strategy accordingly.

Finally, it is important to keep a close eye on your engagement metrics and adjust your strategy as needed. This may involve experimenting with different posting times, using different hashtags, or tweaking the visual elements of your content. By continuously iterating and improving your content strategy, you can build a loyal following on Reels and drive meaningful engagement with your audience.

Measuring Success and Analyzing Performance on Reels:

Measuring the success and analyzing the performance of your content is crucial when it comes to determining the effectiveness of your marketing strategy on Reels. There are various metrics and tools available on the platform to track your performance and make data-driven decisions for future content.

One important metric to track is the number of views, which indicates how many times your Reel has been watched. This metric is particularly important because it helps you gauge the success of your content and identify which types of content are resonating with your audience. Additionally, you can track the engagement rate of your Reels, which includes likes, comments, shares, and saves. This metric is an indication of how engaging and valuable your content is to your audience.

Insights is a built-in tool that allows you to track the performance of your Reels. It provides valuable information on your audience demographics, including age, gender, and location, which can help you tailor your content to your specific audience. You can also track the reach and impressions of your Reels, which helps you determine how many unique users have viewed your content.

One important aspect to keep in mind is that this platform's algorithm takes into account the engagement rate of your content when determining its visibility on users' feeds. This means that the higher the engagement rate, the more likely your content will be shown to a wider audience.

To increase engagement and improve the performance of your Reels, it's important to experiment with different types of content and posting schedules. You can also leverage features, such as interactive stickers, polls, and questions, to encourage your audience to engage with your content.

Furthermore, collaborating with other creators and brands can help increase your reach and exposure on the platform. By partnering with other creators, you can tap into their existing audience and expand your reach to new audiences.

In addition to Insights, there are various third-party analytics tools available that can help you track your performance and gain deeper insights into your audience. These tools can provide more detailed information on engagement, audience demographics, and even competitor analysis.

Overall, measuring the success and analyzing the performance of your Reels is essential to improving your marketing strategy and growing your audience on the platform. By tracking important metrics and experimenting with different types of content, you can increase engagement, reach, and ultimately, revenue on Reels.

Legal and Ethical Considerations for Revenue Generation on Reels:

The world of social media has brought a new wave of opportunities for individuals to generate revenue and build their careers online. Reels, in particular, has become a popular platform for creators to showcase their skills and content and potentially earn money from their efforts. However, with the rise of monetization opportunities comes the need for creators to navigate legal and ethical considerations to avoid potential legal issues and maintain their integrity as content creators.

One important legal consideration for revenue generation on Reels is compliance with the platform's guidelines and terms of service. The platform has strict guidelines regarding what type of content is allowed on their platform, including guidelines on sponsored content and advertising. Creators must adhere to these guidelines and ensure that any sponsored content is clearly labeled as such.

Additionally, creators must comply with advertising laws and regulations in their respective countries. For instance, in the United States, the Federal Trade Commission (FTC) requires that sponsored content be clearly labeled as advertising to ensure transparency for viewers. Failure to comply with these regulations can result in fines or legal action.

Another important consideration is intellectual property rights. Creators must ensure that their content does not infringe on any copyright or trademark laws. This includes obtaining permission to use any third-party content in their Reels and avoiding any use of copyrighted music or images without proper licensing or permission.

Ethical considerations also play a significant role in revenue generation on Reels. Creators must be transparent with their audience about any sponsored content and ensure that their content aligns with their personal values and beliefs. Misleading or dishonest content can damage the creator's reputation and credibility with their audience.

It is also important for creators to consider the potential impact of their content on their audience. This includes avoiding harmful or offensive content and ensuring that their content is inclusive and respectful of all individuals.

To navigate these legal and ethical considerations, creators can seek guidance from legal professionals and industry organizations. The FTC, for example, provides guidelines and resources for sponsored content and advertising. Additionally, organizations such as the Influencer Marketing Council and the Interactive Advertising Bureau offer best practices and standards for ethical advertising and content creation.

In conclusion, while Reels offers an exciting opportunity for revenue generation, creators must navigate legal and ethical considerations to avoid potential legal issues and maintain their integrity as content creators. By adhering to platform guidelines, obtaining proper permissions, and being transparent and honest with their audience, creators can build successful and sustainable careers on Reels.

The Future of Revenue Generation on Reels:

The popularity of Reels has skyrocketed since its launch in 2020. As more and more creators and businesses flock to the platform, it's important to consider the future of revenue generation on Reels.

One trend that is likely to continue is the use of sponsored content and brand partnerships. As creators build their following and increase their influence on the platform, they become more attractive to brands looking to reach their target audience. This can be a lucrative source of revenue for creators, but it's important to maintain transparency and authenticity in sponsored content.

Another potential avenue for revenue generation is the use of in-app purchases. The platform has already introduced shopping tags and the ability to link to products in Reels, but there is room for further development in this area. For example, creators could potentially sell their own merchandise or offer exclusive content to subscribers.

As the platform continues to evolve, there may also be opportunities for creators to monetize their content through subscriptions or membership programs. This could offer a more consistent and reliable source of income compared to sporadic brand partnerships or sponsored content.

Additionally, the integration of augmented reality and virtual reality technologies could open up new possibilities for revenue generation.

For example, creators could potentially sell virtual products or experiences within their Reels content.

However, as the platform evolves and new revenue streams emerge, it's important for creators and businesses to stay aware of the legal and ethical considerations. This includes disclosing sponsored content and complying with advertising regulations, as well as respecting user privacy and data protection laws.

In conclusion, the future of revenue generation on Reels is likely to be shaped by a combination of existing strategies such as sponsored content and brand partnerships, as well as new developments in in-app purchases, subscriptions, and virtual experiences. As the platform continues to evolve, it's important for creators and businesses to stay aware of the legal and ethical considerations and adapt their strategies accordingly.

Reels has undoubtedly become a significant platform for businesses, marketers, and creators to generate revenue. It provides an opportunity to showcase creativity and innovative ideas while reaching a vast and engaged audience. With the increasing competition, it is imperative to utilize the latest strategies, tools, and features to stand out in the marketplace.

As we have discussed in this chapter, there are several ways to generate revenue on Reels, including sponsored content, affiliate marketing, and monetization features like IGTV ads and shopping tags. It is essential to follow best practices for creating engaging content, building a following, and analyzing performance to ensure the success of your revenue-generating efforts.

However, it is equally essential to keep legal and ethical considerations in mind while generating revenue on Reels. As the platform evolves and new features are introduced, it is crucial to stay updated on the latest guidelines and regulations.

The future of revenue generation on Reels looks promising with the platform's continued growth and investment in new features and monetization options. As more businesses and creators join the platform, the competition will undoubtedly increase, making it necessary to stay ahead of the curve with innovative ideas and strategies.

Reels provides an opportunity to reach a vast and engaged audience while generating revenue. By following the best practices, utilizing the latest strategies and features, and staying updated on legal and ethical considerations, businesses and creators can maximize their revenue generation potential on this platform.

SEO: The Backbone of Every Online Business

In today's digital landscape, having a strong online presence is critical for the success of any business. However, simply having a website or social media account is not enough. In order to be truly visible and stand out in the crowded online marketplace, businesses must optimize their content for search engines through Search Engine Optimization (SEO).

SEO is the practice of optimizing a website or online content to improve its ranking and visibility in search engine results pages (SERPs). By incorporating relevant keywords, metadata, and other technical optimizations, businesses can improve their chances of appearing at the top of search results when users search for relevant terms.

In this chapter, we will explore the importance of SEO for businesses operating in various online platforms we have discussed so far. We will delve into the technical aspects of SEO, including keyword research and on-page optimizations, and provide practical advice for businesses to improve their SEO and increase their online visibility. We will also discuss how SEO can drive traffic and revenue for businesses, and explore emerging trends and innovations in the field.

Search engine optimization (SEO) is the practice of optimizing a website or online content to rank higher in search engine results pages (SERPs). The goal of SEO is to increase organic traffic to a website by improving its visibility and relevance to search engine users. SEO involves a variety of techniques, including keyword research, on-page optimization, link building, and content creation.

At its core, SEO is about understanding the search engine algorithms and designing a website that meets their criteria. This includes having a clear site structure, optimizing content for keywords, and building high-quality links from other websites.

Keyword research is a critical part of SEO. By identifying the keywords and phrases that your target audience is searching for, you can optimize your website to better match those queries. This involves analyzing search volume, competition, and relevance to your business.

On-page optimization involves optimizing the content and structure of your website pages to make them more search engine-friendly. This includes optimizing meta titles and descriptions, header tags, image alt tags, and URL structure.

Link building is the process of acquiring backlinks from other websites. Backlinks are important because they signal to search engines that your website is a trusted and authoritative source of information. However, not all backlinks are created equal – quality backlinks from reputable websites are more valuable than spammy or low-quality backlinks.

Content creation is another important aspect of SEO. By creating high-quality, relevant, and engaging content, you can attract more visitors to your website and keep them engaged. This can also help to build your brand reputation and authority in your industry.

In the following sections, we will explore how SEO can be applied to different types of online businesses, including e-commerce websites, blogs, and online marketplaces.

Keyword research is a crucial aspect of SEO that involves identifying the keywords and phrases that your target audience is using to find your products or services. By understanding the keywords that are relevant to your business, you can optimize your website content to ensure it appears in the search engine results pages (SERPs) when people search for those terms.

To conduct effective keyword research, you need to use a combination of tools and techniques. One of the most popular tools for keyword research is Keyword Planner, which allows you to see the search volume and competition level for specific keywords.

There are also several other tools available, such as SEMrush, Ahrefs, and Moz Keyword Explorer, which can provide more detailed insights into keyword trends and competition levels. These tools can help you identify the best keywords to target, as well as identify gaps in your current keyword strategy.

In addition to using keyword research tools, it is also important to conduct competitor analysis to see what keywords your competitors are targeting. This can help you identify opportunities to target keywords that are not being heavily targeted by your competitors.

When conducting keyword research, it is important to keep in mind the intent behind the search terms. For example, a search for "buy shoes" indicates a strong purchase intent, while a search for "how to tie shoelaces" indicates a informational intent. Understanding the intent behind the search terms can help you tailor your content to meet the needs of your audience.

Let's take the example of a small business that sells handmade soaps and wants to improve its website's SEO.

The first step in conducting keyword research is to identify relevant keywords that potential customers might use when searching for handmade soaps. Some possible keywords could include "handmade soap," "natural soap," "organic soap," "vegan soap," "scented soap," and "moisturizing soap."

Once these keywords have been identified, the next step is to determine the search volume and competition level for each keyword. Search volume refers to the number of times a keyword is searched on search engines, while competition level refers to the number of other websites that are also targeting the same keyword.

To conduct this analysis, the small business could use a keyword research tool like Keyword Planner or SEMrush. These tools provide data on search volume and competition level for different keywords, as well as suggestions for related keywords that may be worth targeting.

In analyzing the data, the small business might find that "handmade soap" has high search volume but also high competition, making it difficult to rank for. Meanwhile, "organic soap" has lower search volume but also lower competition, indicating that it may be easier to rank for and could still drive significant traffic to the website.

Based on this analysis, the small business might choose to focus its SEO efforts on targeting keywords like "organic soap" and "vegan soap," which have relatively lower competition but still have significant search volume. The business might also choose to create content that incorporates these keywords, such as blog posts or product descriptions that highlight the organic and vegan ingredients in their handmade soaps.

By conducting thorough keyword research and targeting the right keywords, the small business can improve its website's SEO and attract more potential customers to its online store.

Overall, effective keyword research is essential for optimizing your website for search engines and attracting the right audience to your business. By understanding the keywords that your target audience is using, you can create targeted and relevant content that will help improve your website's ranking in the SERPs.

SEO for E-commerce Businesses:

In today's digital age, e-commerce businesses have become a crucial aspect of the retail industry. With the increasing number of e-commerce platforms, the competition among businesses has become intense. In order to stand out from the competition, it is important for e-commerce businesses to have a strong online presence. One of the most effective ways to achieve this is through search engine optimization (SEO). SEO helps businesses to optimize their website for search engines, increase visibility, and drive more organic traffic. In this section, we will discuss the basics of SEO for e-commerce businesses and how it can help them grow and succeed.

The importance of SEO for e-commerce businesses:

For e-commerce businesses, SEO is essential for driving traffic, increasing brand visibility, and improving conversion rates. With the right SEO strategies, e-commerce businesses can improve their search engine rankings and attract potential customers who are actively searching for their products. This means that businesses can drive more targeted traffic to their website, which is more likely to convert into sales.

Additionally, SEO can help e-commerce businesses to establish their brand and increase their online authority. By optimizing their website and creating high-quality content, businesses can build trust and credibility with their audience. This, in turn, can lead to increased customer loyalty and repeat business.

SEO strategies for e-commerce businesses:

1. Keyword research: One of the most important aspects of SEO for e-commerce businesses is keyword research. This involves identifying the keywords and phrases that potential customers are using to search for products in your industry. By targeting

these keywords in your website content and product descriptions, you can increase your visibility in search results and attract more targeted traffic to your website.

2. On-page optimization: On-page optimization refers to the optimization of individual pages on your website to improve their search engine rankings. This involves optimizing your page titles, meta descriptions, header tags, and content to include your target keywords and provide valuable information to search engines and users.

3. User experience: User experience is a crucial factor in SEO for e-commerce businesses. A website that is easy to navigate, loads quickly, and provides a seamless user experience is more likely to rank well in search results and attract more traffic. This can be achieved through a mobile-friendly design, clear navigation, and fast loading times.

4. Link building: Link building involves acquiring links from other websites back to your own. This can help to increase your website's authority and improve your search engine rankings. For e-commerce businesses, this can be achieved through guest blogging, influencer outreach, and content marketing.

Conclusion:

SEO is a powerful tool for e-commerce businesses that can help them to increase visibility, attract more targeted traffic, and improve their online authority. By implementing the right SEO strategies, e-commerce businesses can establish their brand, build trust with their audience, and ultimately drive more sales.

SEO for Content-Based Businesses:

Content-based businesses, such as blogs, news sites, and other information-based websites, rely heavily on search engine optimization (SEO) to attract traffic and generate revenue. These businesses create content for their audience, and SEO helps ensure that the content is visible and accessible to users searching for related information online.

Keyword Research

Keyword research is an essential aspect of SEO for content-based businesses. By researching and targeting specific keywords, businesses can increase their visibility in search results for relevant queries. To conduct keyword research, businesses can use various tools, such as Keyword Planner, SEMrush, and Ahrefs. These tools provide data on search volume, competition, and related keywords, which can help businesses identify relevant and high-traffic keywords to target in their content.

On-Page Optimization

On-page optimization involves optimizing individual web pages for specific keywords and ensuring that they are structured in a way that is easy for search engines to understand. This includes optimizing titles, headings, meta descriptions, and content. Content-based businesses should also focus on creating high-quality, informative, and engaging content that aligns with their target audience's search intent.

Link Building

Link building is an important aspect of SEO for content-based businesses. Building high-quality backlinks from other reputable websites can increase a website's authority and visibility in search results. Content-based businesses can earn backlinks by creating informative and shareable content that other websites are likely to link to. Guest blogging and influencer outreach are other effective link building strategies.

Technical SEO

Technical SEO involves optimizing the technical aspects of a website to improve its visibility and ranking in search results. This includes ensuring that the website is mobile-friendly, has fast load times, and is structured in a way that is easy for search engines to crawl and understand. Content-based businesses should also use schema markup to provide additional information to search engines about their content.

SEO is a crucial component of success for content-based businesses. By conducting keyword research, optimizing on-page content, building high-quality backlinks, and focusing on technical SEO, businesses can improve their visibility and ranking in search results, attract more traffic, and generate revenue through advertising, affiliate marketing, and other revenue streams.

SEO for Influencers and Vloggers:

SEO (Search Engine Optimization) is crucial for influencers and vloggers who want to grow their online presence and increase their visibility to potential brand partnerships and followers. By optimizing their content for search engines, they can improve their rankings and increase their reach.

The first step in SEO for influencers and vloggers is to conduct keyword research. They need to identify the terms and phrases that their target audience is searching for and incorporate those keywords into their content. This can include using long-tail keywords, which are more specific and targeted, and incorporating them into their titles, descriptions, and tags.

In addition to keyword research, influencers and vloggers should focus on creating high-quality, engaging content that is valuable to their audience. This includes using visually appealing images and videos, providing helpful tips and advice, and sharing personal experiences and stories.

Another important aspect of SEO for influencers and vloggers is building backlinks. Backlinks are links from other websites to their content, which can help increase their credibility and authority with search engines. This can be done by reaching out to other bloggers and influencers in their niche and asking for guest posting opportunities or collaborations.

Social media can also play a role in SEO for influencers and vloggers. By sharing their content on social media platforms and engaging with their followers, they can increase their visibility and reach. It's also important to optimize their social media profiles with relevant keywords and links to their website or other social media profiles.

Lastly, influencers and vloggers should regularly analyze their website and social media analytics to track their performance and identify areas for improvement. This can include monitoring their search engine rankings, website traffic, and social media engagement.

Overall, by implementing SEO best practices, influencers and vloggers can increase their visibility and reach, attract more brand partnerships, and grow their following.

Local SEO for Brick-and-Mortar Businesses:

In the digital age, local businesses need to prioritize their online presence to stay competitive. Local SEO is a strategy that aims to improve the visibility of a business in search engine results for local searches. It involves optimizing a business's website, My Business profile, and other online directories to help it rank higher in local search results.

This section will explore the importance of local SEO for brick-and-mortar businesses and provide practical advice on how to optimize for local search.

Why Local SEO Matters for Brick-and-Mortar Businesses:

Local SEO is critical for brick-and-mortar businesses as it helps them attract local customers who are searching for products or services in their area. When a potential customer searches for a business or service in their locality, they are more likely to visit a store that appears at the top of the search results.

According to some popular company, 46% of all searches have a local intent. This means that people are actively looking for businesses or services near them. By optimizing for local search, brick and mortar businesses can reach these potential customers and increase foot traffic to their stores.

Additionally, local SEO helps businesses build trust and credibility with potential customers. When a business appears at the top of the search results, it signals to customers that it is a trusted and reputable business.

How to Optimize for Local SEO:

Here are some practical tips for optimizing a brick and mortar business's online presence for local search:

Claim and Optimize Your My Business Profile:

My Business is a free tool that helps businesses manage their online presence across internet, including search and maps. By claiming and optimizing a My Business profile, businesses can provide accurate information to potential customers, including their location, hours of operation, website, and contact information.

To optimize a My Business profile, businesses should:

1. Ensure all information is complete and accurate.
2. Use relevant keywords in the business name and description.
3. Add high-quality photos of the business and its products or services.
4. Encourage customers to leave reviews.
5. Optimize Your Website for Local Search:
   To optimize a website for local search, businesses should:
   Include location-specific keywords in the website's content, meta tags, and URLs.
   Ensure the website is mobile-friendly and loads quickly.
   Add a map and directions to the business's location.
   Include customer reviews and testimonials on the website.

6. Get Listed on Online Directories:
   Getting listed on online directories can help improve a business's visibility in local search results. Businesses should ensure their information is consistent and accurate across all online directories, including Yelp, Yellow Pages, and TripAdvisor.
7. Create Local Content:
   Creating local content can help businesses rank higher in local search results. This can include blog posts, videos, or social media content that highlights the business's connection to the local community.

Local SEO is a critical strategy for brick-and-mortar businesses to attract local customers and improve their online visibility. By claiming and optimizing their My Business profile, optimizing their website for local search, getting listed on online directories, and creating local content, businesses can improve their local search rankings and attract more foot traffic to their stores.

Search engine optimization (SEO) has been a critical aspect of online business for many years, and it has evolved significantly over time. As search engines continue to refine their algorithms and technology advances, the landscape of SEO is constantly changing. In this chapter, we will explore the future of SEO and how businesses can prepare for the upcoming changes.

1. The Role of Artificial Intelligence (AI) in SEO:
   As AI technology continues to advance, it is becoming increasingly important in the world of SEO. Search engines are now able to analyze and understand content at a deeper level, allowing them to provide more relevant and accurate results to users. This means that businesses must focus on creating high-quality, engaging content that aligns with their target audience's needs and preferences.
   AI is also being used to identify and penalize black hat SEO tactics, such as keyword stuffing and link spamming. This means that businesses must ensure that their SEO practices are ethical

and align with best practices to avoid penalties and maintain a positive online reputation.

2. The Rise of Voice Search:

Voice search has become increasingly popular in recent years, thanks to the rise of digital assistants. As more people rely on voice search to find information, businesses must optimize their content for voice search queries.

This means that businesses must focus on creating content that is conversational in nature and aligns with the way people naturally speak. Long-tail keywords and natural language phrases are becoming increasingly important for optimizing content for voice search. Additionally, businesses must ensure that their website is optimized for mobile devices, as many voice searches are conducted through mobile devices.

3. The Importance of User Experience:

As search engines continue to prioritize user experience, businesses must focus on providing a seamless, engaging experience for their website visitors. This means optimizing for fast page load times, ensuring that the website is mobile-friendly, and creating content that is easy to navigate and consume.

User experience is also becoming increasingly important for search engine rankings. Search engines are now able to measure user engagement metrics like bounce rate and time on site, which can impact search rankings. Businesses must focus on providing high-quality content and a positive user experience to improve their search rankings.

4. The Impact of Visual Search:

Visual search is an emerging trend that is expected to have a significant impact on SEO in the future. Visual search technology allows users to search for information using images rather than text. This means that businesses must focus on optimizing their images for search engines, including adding descriptive alt tags and captions.

Additionally, businesses must ensure that their website is optimized for visual search, including ensuring that images are properly sized and formatted for optimal viewing on different devices.

SEO is an ever-evolving field, and businesses must stay up-to-date with the latest trends and technologies to stay ahead of the competition. By focusing on creating high-quality content, optimizing for voice and visual search, prioritizing user experience, and aligning with ethical SEO practices, businesses can position themselves for success in the future of SEO.

Conclusion

As the online marketplace continues to grow and evolve, businesses must adapt and innovate to remain competitive. The strategies and practices discussed in this book provide a foundation for success in the digital age.

From building a strong online presence and standing out in a crowded market to utilizing the latest technologies and trends, businesses can leverage the power of the internet to reach a global audience and drive growth.

However, with these opportunities come challenges, such as increased competition, the need for authenticity and ethical considerations, and the ever-changing landscape of the online marketplace.

By following the best practices and staying up to date with emerging trends and technologies, businesses can not only survive but thrive in this dynamic and exciting space.

It's crucial for businesses to understand the importance of customer experience, effective branding, and exceptional customer service. A positive reputation and engagement with customers can make all the difference in driving sales and building a loyal customer base.

In addition, businesses must keep up with the fast-paced nature of the online marketplace, from the rise of short-form video content to the emergence of new freelance marketplaces. It's important to embrace innovation and adapt to change to stay ahead of the competition.

SEO is another critical component of a successful online strategy. Understanding the basics of SEO and conducting thorough keyword research can improve a business's visibility in search engine rankings, leading to increased traffic and sales.

Overall, the online marketplace presents vast opportunities for businesses of all sizes and industries. By leveraging the power of technology and staying on top of industry trends, businesses can succeed and thrive in the digital age.

In conclusion, the online marketplace is constantly evolving, and businesses must be adaptable and innovative to stay ahead. By utilizing the strategies and best practices outlined in this book, businesses can build a strong online presence, stand out in a crowded market, and drive revenue growth. The future of business is digital, and those who are prepared to embrace it will be the ones who succeed.